THREE YEARS
AT SEA

A FAMILY'S ADVENTURE
OF DISCOVERY AND DANGER

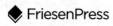 FriesenPress

Suite 300 - 990 Fort St
Victoria, BC, Canada, V8V 3K2
www.friesenpress.com

ISBN
978-1-4602-7389-0 (Paperback)
978-1-4602-7390-6 (eBook)

1. Biography & Autobiography, Personal Memoirs

Distributed to the trade by The Ingram Book Company

Table of Contents

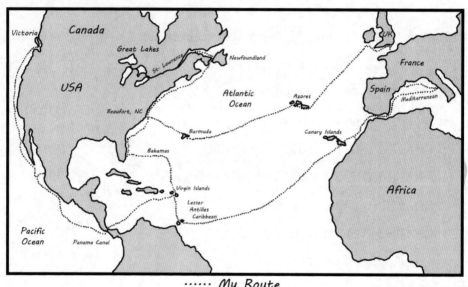

Prologue

With a diagnosis of hepatitis and the threat of death, suddenly one is left to wonder what life's journey is all about. Bill had a promising career with a large company and was being groomed to climb the corporate ladder, when tragically in the summer of 1974, hepatitis struck, and he was rushed to hospital.

Recovery had left him weak, yet he was grateful to be alive; the realization that he had survived the operation had given him a new appreciation for life.

The previous summer, I had returned to Ottawa for my tenth nursing reunion and went sailing with some friends on their 26-foot Thunderbird. When I got home, I was anxious to talk to Bill about what a great experience it had been. Unknown to me, Bill had also gone sailing with a friend on his 26-foot Thunderbird. We agreed that we wanted to do some sailing while living in Vancouver and it was almost as if fate had shown us a new way of life, a new freedom away from boardrooms and hospital wards.

Bill's life had been hanging in the balance and now he had been given a second chance. With the prospect of a journey of adventure, we were ready to embark upon a wonderful experience, and so began a new chapter in our lives.

Pat Hapgood

Dedication

In loving memory of Mike Butorac, who kept constant contact with us by letters, audio tapes, and phone calls whenever possible, and always assured us we were doing the right thing.

CHAPTER 1

Leading up to Our Sailing Adventure

"The person who goes farthest is generally the one who is willing to do and dare. The sure-thing boat never gets far from shore."

– Dale Carnegie

Even before the children were born, my wife Pat and I had been avid campers. We lived in Ajax, Ontario, in central Canada, and frequently camped at Algonquin Park for long weekends with friends. An evening by the fire was always cherished and was a welcome relief after a hectic week at work.

Suddenly, there was a change in our lives. An opportunity arose for me to accept a position in Vancouver, British Columbia, which meant having to leave behind family and many friends in Ontario. Having two young daughters, Julie, age three, and Jennifer, age one, it was going to be a big adjustment for Pat, as her life was going to be looking after two daughters in a city where she didn't know anyone. It would be different for me, however, because my work involved interaction with lots of people. I had been quite involved in sports car racing in Ontario and Quebec, winning the class championship in 1970. I would be leaving this behind.

So, finally, in January 1971, we left our home in Ajax, a short distance from Toronto. Pat drove our car, and I drove our van, towing my racing car on a trailer.

Once spring came in beautiful British Columbia, it was back to camping and exploring our new countryside. After only two years of this, there was dramatic change in our lives.

On a drive up the Sunshine Coast to our favourite camping ground at Alice Lake, we were enthralled by the many islands off the coast, most of which were accessible only by boat. We wondered what it would be like to explore these islands, so we discussed the possibility of having our own boat.

Upon our return home, we scanned the papers, contacted brokers, and visited marinas. It didn't take long for us to realize that we couldn't afford what we wanted. *But what if we built it?* If so, then perhaps we could afford it.

It was decided! We bought a boat kit: a Swiftsure 24. The hull and deck were bonded, so it was simply a matter of building the galley, head, holding tank, berths, bulkheads, a settee, a dining table, a mast, boom, spinnaker pole, rudder, tiller, and rigging. Then we had to install a motor, fuel tanks, water tanks and then get the sails.

Well, in May 1974, after seven months of toiling every night after work and every weekend and spending a lot of money, we launched our boat, *Melissa*, which we named after my grandmother. My grandparents had played a big part in my early life. My grandfather, Ned, had been a boat builder, but I didn't think Ned was a very romantic name for a boat, so we christened her *Melissa*.

Now that the boat was built, all we had to do was learn how to sail. Pat took the Power Squadron course, and I read every book on sailing I could get my hands on. Power Squadron almost ruined our relationship. "Whadayamean true north? Our compass doesn't point to true north. We are going to use magnetic north." "But in the Power Squadron book—" and so on. Pat took a supreme interest in the course and became proficient in reading charts and learning seafaring etiquette.

We joined the Tsawwassen Yacht Club and went out racing every Wednesday night and, in spite of our high-performance-oriented Swiftsure 24, we came dead last. By watching what our competitors were doing, we gradually caught on, and it opened up a new world for us. Throughout the summer we sailed every weekend; across the Strait of Georgia, to Galliano Island, Pender Island, Cabbage Island, and the San Juan Islands.

By August of that year, we decided to take a sailing vacation up to Desolation Sound. The trip was breath-taking and upon our arrival we discovered a quiet little anchorage at Mink Island where another boat was anchored. As I was setting out our anchor our neighbor called out to me and informed me that I should tie a shoreline as the tide was strong and the bay was quite shallow.

Is that a Swiftsure 24?" he asked.

"Yes," I replied. "Is that an Ericson 29?"

The man nodded and then suggested that once I'd anchored, to go over for a chat. After further discussion, he inquired how much I would be willing to accept for *Melissa*. I informed him that I would accept $12,000 to which he told me that he would accept $20,000 for his Ericson 29.

I took a moment to consider his offer and, after acknowledging that I would pay him a further $8,000, we shook on the deal.

After returning from our vacation, I drove to Kelowna and met him for lunch at his golf club, and gave him a certified cheque for $8,000. The boat was then moored at False Creek Marina in Vancouver, which we then renamed *Melissa II*. Looking back, I can hardly believe that things turned out that way.

During the winter, we sailed most weekends and took a three-week cruise at Christmas time. We feasted on freshly caught salmon and crabs. Even though it was winter, it didn't squelch our enthusiasm for sailing.

In the spring of 1976, I flew to Toronto, Ontario, and accepted a business position that required me to relocate to that area by September. We decided to have a last west coast cruise before our departure and took our daughters out of school at the beginning of June and headed off for a three-month sailing adventure to Alaska. From Ketchikan, we sailed over to the Queen Charlotte Islands and returned home by skirting the west side of Vancouver Island. We lived on fish, mussels, pork, beans, and rice. Continuous rain didn't dampen our enthusiasm for exploring the rugged terrain of the stunning north-west coast.

While en route, we made a brave decision to have friends search out a house for us in Whitby, which is a short distance from Toronto. We appointed a lawyer in Prince Rupert to complete the paperwork on a place that we hadn't even seen, something that concerned our family and friends, who questioned our sanity. It wasn't until September that we arrived back in Vancouver, ending our trip of three months and over 2,000 nautical miles. After arranging to have *Melissa II* shipped back to Lake Ontario, we loaded our furniture and belongings onto a rented truck and set off on a three-day drive across the country. It was sad for us to say goodbye to our friends, but we told them that we would return.

When we arrived in Whitby, we picked up the keys from a friend who had helped with the transaction and inspected our new home. *It was perfect!* It fit our needs. It was fun re-uniting with old Ontario friends and making new ones. We joined the Whitby Yacht Club and made arrangements for launching our boat when it arrived. It was only in the water for six weeks when we had to haul it out for the winter, something we weren't used to doing, as we had sailed all winter long in Vancouver.

We had a great life in our new home; however, Spring couldn't come quick enough. We launched the boat and got back to sailing as soon as we could, doing a lot of cruising as well as racing. In fact, we entered the Oshawa Clipper race two years in a row; finishing third on one occasion and then came first the following year. We also scored well in the Wednesday evening club racing at the Whitby Yacht Club. Our cruising plans included taking a month's vacation in July to sail to the North Channel in Lake Huron. Our fellow club members questioned that we would sail twenty-four hours a day for four days to reach our destination, but it seemed perfectly normal to us. We had good winds most of the way, using our motor only to transverse the eight locks of the Welland Canal as well as the Detroit and St. Clair Rivers. Then it was back to sailing Lake Huron to the North Channel. *What great cruising grounds!* There were lots of rocky islands covered with wild blueberries for our breakfast pancakes. The water was warm for swimming and was even safe for drinking. We enjoyed the area so much that we did it again the following year in 1978.

Two years later, who would have guessed the outcome of Pat's trip to the hospital to visit me on March 22, 1979? It was her birthday, and I was there recovering from surgery to repair a broken shoulder from a cross-country ski racing accident. As she sat on the edge of my hospital bed, she agreed when I said that we should forget about buying a bigger boat and just go with what we had. Months earlier we had discussed the eventual return to British Columbia.

Our destination was Victoria on Vancouver Island, and we had decided to take about three years to do the trip; we would sail out the St. Lawrence River and work our way down to the Caribbean. The thought of crossing the Atlantic hadn't entered into the picture at that point. There was going to be lots of offshore sailing, so we would have to get ourselves familiar with using a sextant for celestial navigation. Within two months we had sold our cars, put the house up for sale, arranged to auction off all our furniture and started preparing the boat for our departure. We were aiming to leave at the end of June when the children got out of school.

We enjoyed racing *Melissa II* and were fortunate enough to win many flags (i.e., trophies). That is what convinced us that she would be an ideal world cruiser. She was fast, nimble, and easy to sail and well-built to handle the stresses likely to be encountered on ocean passages. An Ericson 29, she was twenty-nine feet long and nine feet wide, built in 1974. Ours had a tall rig, which classified it as an IOR half-ton racing boat, which has nothing to do with the boat's weight, but signifies its racing class. She was not unlike the majority of sailboats found at a marina. Our complement of sails included everything from a storm jib to a 180% genoa and a spinnaker.

The mainsail had two reefing points, and we had a storm trysail for those really strong winds in excess of 40 knots. We had a folding propeller to reduce drag when underway by sail. Our engine was an Atomic 4 (4 cylinder, 30 horsepower). I had strengthened all our stays to ensure the best protection for our mast. Our ground tackle consisted of a forty-five-pound CQR anchor with 200 feet of chain and a stern anchor, a thirteen-pound Danforth tethered to fifty feet of chain and 300 feet of yacht braid. For emergencies, we had an extra 1,000 feet of half-inch yacht braid, which was stored in an aft locker. Maybe we went a bit of overboard (no pun intended), but interestingly enough, we had occasion to use all of our ground tackle and the 1,000 feet of line more than once. In fact, I can say that it saved our lives and our boat. I had added an extra fuel tank and increased water capacity to 80 gallons. I should mention that when I say miles, I mean nautical miles, 6,076 feet or 1,852 metres. Also, I always refer to wind speed or boat speed in knots; 1 knot is 1.15078 mph.

Before departing, we had to look after several practicalities: education for the children, health insurance, boat insurance, etc. We found a suitable correspondence course for the girls and arranged for health insurance. We looked at a number of options for school for Julie and Jennifer, finally deciding on a correspondence program offered by the Ontario Government. It had been developed for children who lived in isolated communities in Northern Canada. It entailed weekly assignments to be mailed in, and all of the material was issued for the whole year, which would prove to be a problem when travelling on a small boat and continually on the move. Our kind friends, Craig and Joyce Gillespie from Vineland, Ontario, agreed to look after our mail and finances. Offshore boat insurance is extremely expensive, and the question was raised that if we lost the boat with all hands, who would be around to collect it? So, we decided against getting it; instead, I would ensure the safety of my family at all times.

CHAPTER 2

Underway at Last

"He that will not sail till all dangers are over must never put to sea."

– Dr. Thomas Fuller

On July 2, 1979, at 0435 hours, we threw off our lines and departed from the Whitby Yacht Club, leaving behind many friends who we were unlikely to see again for years to come. Naturally, we had anticipated that, yet hadn't considered the level of emotion involved, leaving it too late to question whether we were doing the right thing. We had to just focus on what lay ahead.

Fully laden and ready for the Atlantic

For the first couple of hours, it was foggy and there was little wind. Lake Ontario looked pretty bleak. Then the winds came up behind us, the skies cleared, we set the spinnaker and were moving along at a comfortable 5 to 6 knots, heading east on Lake Ontario. We transversed the Murray Canal into the Bay of Quinte, visiting friends in Belleville. While there, we went to the theatre and saw the movie *Jaws*. I swore I would never get in the water again after that. However, here we were on our way to the Virgin Islands, the best snorkeling waters in the world. From there it was on to Kingston and the mouth of the St. Lawrence River. Now we had wind and current in our favour but often needed help from the Iron Jenny (motor).

The route through the Thousand Islands was full of beauty, but we felt an urgency to get underway. The constant socializing was hard to resist. We enjoyed many layovers along the way: the Royal St. Lawrence Yacht Club at Dorval; the Club Nautique at Rivière-du-Loup, and then finally the Québec Yacht Club.

We began to experience tides at Trois-Rivières, starting with a tide change of only six inches, but increasing to a peak of sixteen feet at Québec City. At that point the river started to widen out, eventually becoming the Gulf of St. Lawrence. Québec or *Kébec* was an Algonquin word meaning "where the river narrows." We celebrated the fact that we had travelled 422 nautical miles from Whitby, Ontario. The last day had been a tough one, with brutal headwinds. The speed indicated on our knot meter went down below 2 knots at times, but we were driven by a current of 6 knots at Richelieu Rapids. In spite of the headwinds, we covered eighty miles in thirteen hours. From there eastward, it was like the open ocean. The cold fresh water from the Saguenay and the warmer salty water of the St. Lawrence meet to create a rich marine environment. The rivers support an abundance of krill, making the area very attractive for whales – beluga, minke, humpback and fin. We began to see beluga whales at the mouth of the Saguenay River, and we could taste the salt from the splashes of water on our faces.

We continued high on the Québec North Shore. It was safe to sail twenty-four hours a day now because it was like sailing in the open ocean. Julie and I would be on watch for two hours then switch with Pat and Jennifer for their two hours. We reached Baie-Trinité, a little settlement on the Quebec North Shore. In fact, that is where I was born. My dad was a forester from New Hampshire who had been sent there to oversee a lumbering operation. To make it enticing for him to relocate, the company built a beautiful waterfront home for him, the one in which I was born. They also built a tennis court for my mother, who was an amateur tennis star at the time. This was in the early 1930s. Imagine a company doing that for an employee today! With no road access to Baie-Trinité, the only way in was by boat or airplane. The company often flew in some of mother's friends to play tennis. The house is now the staff house for company guests and has a portrait of my dad over the fireplace. My mother and my step-father, George, who lived in Arizona, came to Baie-Trinité to wish us "bon voyage." We had a great lobster feast and met people who remembered my dad, who died in 1955 at age forty-six. My recollection of Baie-Trinité was vague to say the least, as we had moved to Trois-Rivières when I was nine months old. I think I was the only Anglo-Saxon born there.

It was sad saying our goodbyes, as we weren't sure when we were going to see my mother and George again. As it turned out, it was more than three years later when we rendezvoused in San Francisco near the completion of our adventure.

We saw five or six whales daily after leaving Tadoussac. In fact, I had a fear of running into them on our overnight sailing, a fear I maintained throughout the entire trip. Incidentally, an Australian couple we met in Tobago three years later thought I was crazy to have such a fear, but we heard from them later that they had been struck by a whale near Tahiti en route home. Their rudder was severely damaged, and the boat had to be hauled for repairs. In a few instances, sailing cruisers have been sunk by whales. As described in their book, *Survive the Savage Sea*, the Robertson family were sunk by killer whales. A Florida couple's sailboat was sunk by whales off Costa Rica, and they survived sixty-six days at sea by eating raw fish. The Baileys wrote the book *117 Days Adrift*, after their boat was sunk by a whale; so you see, my fear wasn't unfounded.

Our next anchorage was at Ellis Bay on Anticosti Island, which we fetched about 0700 hours on July 24, 1979. After entering the harbour, we headed for the government dock and saw that there were three boats displaying Québec flags on their stern. We were flying the Canadian flag, of course and the crew of the three boats got up on the wharf and turned their backs on us. We got the message so we settled for anchoring in an open roadstead and endured rough seas all night long.

The following morning, we had pancakes for breakfast and then headed for Rivière-au-Renard (Fox River), Gaspé. We didn't see any foxes, but we did see a shoreline of fish guts and garbage. People on the dock had no hesitation about throwing garbage in the water. We visited the Coast Guard Station, and they were very helpful with tide and weather information for us to assist in making our next port, Prince Edward Island (P.E.I.), which was about 200 miles away. We departed at 0445 hours, passing Percé Rock just around noon, giving us a great opportunity to take pictures. We rounded North Point Light at the easterly tip of P.E.I. at midnight and continued on to Darnley Basin. This east side of the island is not only very shallow, but is exposed to the north-east swells that break on the sandy shoals, making landfalls virtually impossible for all but the local fishermen. Darn hard to navigate, this is why they probably call it Darnley Basin. Fortunately, Little Scottie, a local fisherman, led us in and threw us a big fresh cod when we anchored. We were now 1,000 nautical miles from Whitby.

We loved P.E.I. In Summerside; we stayed with family and Pat's mother flew in from Ottawa to join us. We visited Woodleigh Replicas, a twenty-five-acre site of replicas of St. Paul's Cathedral, Anne Hathaway's cottage, Shakespeare's birthplace, The Old Curiosity Shop, and Dunvegan Castle, as well as a replica of the Tower of London, which covers a substantial portion of the site. We spent a day at Cavendish Beach and Avonlea, the village of *Anne of Green Gables*. We made a lot of friends at the Summerside Yacht Club. They asked me to give my slide presentation on our trip, *Sailing the Pacific Coast to Alaska*, and they were amazed at my photos of the west coast. During my daily morning run, I met Gerard MacPhee, a local dentist, and had dinner with him and his wife, Sue. Jennifer needed some dental work done, which he did at no charge. He asked me, "Do you want to go out on a commercial fishing boat for the day?" I left at 0230 hours to meet his brother, Francis, a commercial fisherman in Souris at the east end of the Island, and his crew member, Art Peters. We went pair fishing on *Black Diamond*. Pair fishing is where two boats string a net between them and winch it slowly in throughout the day. We caught 11,000 pounds of cod and hake. Art, a gourmet cook, served roast beef for lunch, even though we had just finished a huge breakfast. We didn't come in until 2100 hours, but the day went fast and we laughed constantly. I'm so grateful to have had the opportunity for this experience.

After departing Darnley Harbour, we headed for Souris, as Francis had suggested we anchor in the harbour to visit for a few days. He was trying to convince me to abandon our trip and take up fishing for a living, assuring me he could find me a boat. It was a very kind offer, but we had a journey to complete.

Upon our arrival at Souris, Jennifer fell off the boat as she was stepping across to the dock. The water was not very clean, and her long blond hair was full of algae and fish guts. Fortunately Francis insisted she come and shower at his home. We had tied up against the harbour wall, and when the fishing fleet came home at the end of each day, they tossed us a fresh cod or hake for our dinner. The time spent in Souris had been wonderful. We had spent most evenings playing cards with wharf mongers and Francis' children became close friends with the girls. It was a sad day when we finally said our goodbyes.

reeling in the net on the Black Diamond

not a bad haul

August 17, 1979, 0600 hours, we departed Souris bound for the Canso Strait, separating Cape Breton from the rest of Nova Scotia. We fetched Port

Hawkesbury halfway through the Strait at 1800 hours and went for an evening walk in town. The people were so friendly and while it was tempting to stay another day, we decided to move on with our journey. At 0600 hours we left for New Harbour Cove, tying up at the dock at 1730 hours. People were curious as to our presence, and came down to check us out, including a couple from Halifax, Wilf and Audrey, who insisted that we call them on arriving in Halifax.

Nova Scotia was not to be outdone by P.E.I. *What friendly people!* We seemed to be adopted by a family in every port. In fact, we were beginning to think we were looking a bit hard done by, as people would insist that we went to their home to bathe, feed us and even do our laundry. Interestingly enough, the majority of these people were non-boaters; however, their generosity was overwhelming.

Nova Scotia, the land of the schooners but not all schoo-
ners are as long as the Bluenose

There is a lot to see and do in Halifax. *What a great place!* The Armdale Yacht Club was very gracious. Their services were wonderful, and the members so friendly. We stayed there for five days, tending to the many boat chores that were accumulating. We began noticing the number of schooner-rigged boats at anchor. It is something you seldom see on the Great Lakes or the west coast. Our eagerness to get on with the voyage was delayed slightly when we reached Lunenburg—more Nova Scotia hospitality, which served us well given the imminent arrival of Hurricane David.

When *Bluenose II* came into port, her crew gave us the Cook's tour of this majestic ship. *Did you know that she once logged 18 knots for an hour and a half?* In town we met many of the craftsmen who had shaped her and a few who had worked on the original *Bluenose*, which in 1946 met its fate on a reef off the coast of Haiti.

It was now well into September and the hurricane season was petering out; so it was time to head south, but not before another layover at Indian Point, still in Nova Scotia. Cousin Ned had arranged a mooring for us and took us to his Kemptville home. Using his metal lathe, we were able to complete a wind-activated self-steering mechanism I was building. It used a 'barn door rudder', activated by a wind vane. There were a lot of metal components that we were able to fabricate with Ned's metal lathe. From that day on, I always referred to my self-steering as Ned. We enjoyed a pleasant three-day visit before heading back to our boat to continue our adventure.

It started with a dreadful three-day passage cutting across the Bay of Fundy, known for its tides, the highest in the world reaching over fifty feet. The winds were howling, and we spent six hours hove to. We were being set north at a rate of 4 knots towards shore with the current of a rising tide. In a full-force gale we made our landfall in Portland, Maine, feeling very grateful that we hadn't suffered any damage. The seventy-foot fishing vessel *Holy Cross* was not so lucky. She reported taking on water very near us, but before anyone was able to locate her, she sank. It was, however, a great relief to hear that her crew took to lifeboats and were rescued within two hours of her sinking.

The Centre Board Yacht Club of Portland did everything possible to make our stay exceptional. We presented them with a club burgee from the Whitby

Yacht Club, as we did with all the yacht clubs we visited. They presented us with one of theirs, which we sent back to Whitby, as we had been doing. Whitby had given us about twenty burgees, which we were proud to pass on to clubs we visited. Carrying on south of Portland, we passed through one cruising haven after another: Annisquam Canal, Marblehead, Cape Cod (where Pat and I had spent our honeymoon), Nantucket, Martha's Vineyard, Newport, Block Island Sound and Long Island Sound, all of which are missed if you take the inland canal route.

Our layover in Newport was another highlight but not the Newport Yacht Club. They wouldn't let us tie up at their 200 feet of dock that was empty. We tied up at the city pier, where we saw the *Enterprise, Intrepid, France 3* and other America's Cup contenders practicing for the 1980 race. They were hauled out of the water daily and polished before heading out for practice each day.

Americas Cup contenders, Enterprise & Intrepid

We saw friends we had first met in Tadoussac. It is amazing how small the world of sailing is. Going in and out of the harbour were visions that you would seldom see anywhere else. Imagine the astonishment of seeing a fully rigged, bark under full sail, *seven* feet long. Her owner and, I am sure, her builder had a faraway look in his eye as if he were still days away from the 'New World' with his scurvy-ridden crew.

Fully rigged and screaming ahead at 2 knots

Mystic Seaport was delightful. After entering the harbour, we waited for the drawbridge to let us into the historic harbour, which consisted of a village with ships and seventeen acres of exhibits depicting coastal life in New England in the 19th century. The *Rose* and the *Joseph Conrad* were tied up at the dock. Even the clinker-built dinghies dated back to those used in the mid-1800s.

Just as we left Mystic Seaport, we got quite a scare. Pat was on watch, and she yelled for me to come up to the cockpit. She pointed to a marker that wasn't on the chart, and it appeared to be moving. It was a periscope! Gradually we saw the conning tower emerge and then the sub surfaced not more than 200 feet away. *It scared the daylights out of us! It crossed our bow!* They obviously took great delight in giving us a fright.

We hadn't planned to dock in New York, but we were running short of supplies. After tying up at a dock on the East River, we found a grocery store and a Laundromat. We only stayed overnight, departing on a foggy morning past the Statue of Liberty and heading south to Delaware City. When we motored away from New York City, our engine started to run roughly. I rinsed out the inline gas filter and checked the carburetor, the distributor, and then the points, but found nothing suspicious. I finally narrowed it down to the coil. All of this I did under sail, which had not been an easy task. Fortunately, my diagnosis was correct, and we got a new coil at the marina at Worton Creek, our next stop. It solved the problem!

The cold weather spurred us along rapidly to the Chesapeake where we feasted on Beautiful Summer (blue crab). We reveled in the history that helped shape the American dream. Baltimore, which was the capital city of the United States in 1777, was the site of the Battle of Baltimore during the War of 1812, where they resisted defeat from the British. A survivor of the battle wrote a poem, calling it *The Star Spangled-Banner*. It became the American national anthem in 1931. Baltimore had some bad times too, as it experienced many riots and a serious fire in 1904. Fortunately, our time there had been a pleasant experience; we had a wonderful time exploring the downtown area, although we did happen to wander a little away from our safety zone, and were warned by a fireman passing by that we should turn back immediately. We did as he instructed, and hightailed it back to the boat.

A snowfall rudely interrupted our stay, so off we went along the coast to Oriental, North Carolina, a small town named after the ship *Oriental* that met her fate in 1862, running aground just north of Cape Hatteras. After tying up at the municipal dock we asked the waitress at the marina restaurant where we might find a grocery store. She was about eighteen years old, and she asked us where we were parked. When we told her that we were walking, she insisted we take her car. We were overwhelmed with her generosity; however, we really wanted a walk after spending so much time on the boat. Even the dogs in Oriental are friendly! A yellow Labrador followed us to the grocery store and waited for us just outside the exit door, about sixty feet from the entrance where we left him. No doubt he had done this before, he knew that we would eventually appear at the exit. The Labrador followed us home and lay down on the dock beside our boat. He was gone the following morning.

Our next stop was Beaufort, North Carolina, which over a period of time became our second home. It is strategically located in the inner banks region between Cape Lookout on the north and Cape Fear on the south. In 2012, Beaufort was ranked as "America's Coolest Small Town" by readers of *Budget Travel Magazine*. Anyone departing from here under sail will find themselves well clear of the dreaded Cape Hatteras, which is characterized by two major Atlantic currents that collide: the southerly flowing cold-water Labrador Current, and the northerly flowing warm-water Florida Current, the Gulf Stream. The collision of two major currents creates turbulent waters and a large expanse of shallow sandbars extending up to fourteen miles (twenty-three kilometers) offshore. The town is home to the North Carolina Maritime Museum, which we became very familiar with. Charles McNeil, the curator, was a boon to offshore sailors, organizing navigation seminars for them and posting up-to-date weather information for routes across the Atlantic. He and his gracious staff became close friends. The museum had a truck that was available for sailors to pick up supplies for their voyage. It also had charts for virtually anywhere in the world. We acquired all the charts we needed for the Bahamas and the Caribbean.

There were many boats in the harbour headed to the Virgin Islands. Rick and Annette Whittaker, with Boson the cat, on *Sauterelle* had been living in Ohio and were bound for the Virgin Islands and then Vancouver, British Columbia. We ran into them time and again and there were others, too, that we continued to meet throughout our journey. On reflection, it was quite amazing how we kept accidentally running into these people at anchorages along the way.

CHAPTER 3
The Sea Beckons Us

"Never in my life before have I experienced such beauty, and fear at the same time."

– Ellen MacArthur

We were in Beaufort for almost three weeks before we departed for the Caribbean on November 7, 1979. The winds were light, and the sky was clear. We were going to be encountering the Gulf Stream for the first time and really didn't know what to expect. Our tactic was to head ESE until we were 150 nautical miles south of Bermuda, then reach south with the trade winds, which are predominately from the east and would be on our port bow, and finally swing south for the last 700 miles to St. Thomas, US Virgin Islands.

By the third day, we had crossed the Gulf Stream, about one hundred miles wide at this point, and we were beating in light northeast winds. The water was warm, and the seas were erratic, indicating that we had reached the Gulf Stream. Our first couple of days had been okay. Early evening we communicated with the vessel *Marconi Conveyor* of Monrovia. She gave us our position, which was forty-five miles further than my dead-reckoning position indicated. My afternoon sun shot I had taken with my sextant pretty much agreed with her. The current had pushed us in a favourable direction. Winds of 20 to 30 knots were predicted for the next day. I was feeling a bit woozy, but I think it was nerves more than seasickness. My sextant shots put us below 32 degrees latitude. We had to get further east before we could veer south to catch the trade winds and carry on down to the Virgin Islands.

As the day progressed, the sky took on a menacing appearance! It was like nothing we had ever seen before. By late afternoon, the winds veered to the south-east and low-lying clouds bunched up like big black mushrooms. *It was frightening!* The wind had piped up, and we were sailing east under double-reefed main and working jib. Suddenly the sky blackened, and we got nailed by a horrendous squall. The jib burst to ribbons on the first gust, and I scrambled forward to take it down and put up the storm jib. I worked my way back to the cockpit when we were smitten by a huge square wave. It hit with such force that it fractured the chain locker bulkhead and put a line of stress cracks along the deck head. I went forward and dropped the storm jib. Pat put the helm over, and we started surfing down the waves, pegging the knot meter at 12 knots under bare poles. The stern was lifting, and we slid down with green water coming over the bow at each trough. It was absolute terror! The winds screamed and the waves were coming at us at about 20 knots and were about thirty feet high and very steep. As near as I could estimate, they were about 500 feet from crest to crest. Our fear was of pitch poling, in other words, "going ass over tea kettle."

In an effort to slow us down, we threw out our 1,000 feet of half-inch yacht braid secured to the winch. It tightened up like a banjo string, slowing us down to 4 or 5 knots, sliding down the waves with no sails. Then we did what we shouldn't have done. We sat with our backs to the bulkhead watching each wave crash into the cockpit. Poor Jennifer was down in the cabin crying that she wanted her Granma. Jennifer suffered the most on passages but glowed with enthusiasm when we made a landfall. Pat and I spelled each other off and on the helm every hour, as we didn't feel comfortable relying on our wind-activated self-steering in following winds.

After fifteen hours, the wind dropped but was still in excess of 40 knots with gusts up to 50 (force 9 and 10 on the Beaufort scale, which has nothing to do with Beaufort, NC, but was named after Frances Beaufort, an ancient mariner). The waves strung out with a greater distance between them and were not as ferocious as they had been. *Melissa II* was doing a lot of flexing, but she had convinced us she was going to take us safely through it. The next day, we were completely exhausted and starved, as we hadn't eaten. *Julie saved the day!* She opened the hatch and passed us a can of peaches. By the evening, the wind had dropped down to force 7, and the seas had settled down to fifteen feet.

Already south of Bermuda, we chose to engage the self-steering and work our way west. We had been keeping track of course changes and speed. It put our DR (dead reckoning) just north of Cape Fear, well clear of Cape Hatteras, which can be extremely dangerous. We were confident that we could avoid it and reach into Beaufort from whence we came. The thought of altering course for the Virgin Islands was not an option because we had boat and sails to repair. The winds were becoming more manageable. We were able to set a double-reefed main with the storm jib. I took a series of sun shots that confirmed our position, so with our tail between our legs, we went back into the port that we had left six days earlier. Feeling discouraged, we were fortunate enough to have friends there who were eager to console us. *But now what?* The new plan was to follow the coast down to Florida, cross over to Freeport, Bahamas, and work our way east until we were almost due north of the Virgin Islands. We spent three long days effecting repairs that were a little more extensive than we had judged. Fortunately, Omar the sail maker was able to repair our sails immediately.

Julie and Jennifer had heard all kinds of stories about the Bermuda Triangle. They asked me if all of this folklore was the cause of our experience. *No!* I explained to them that this area has the highest concentration of cruise ships, commercial ships and pleasure craft in the world. Therefore, you would expect the incidence of mishaps to be much greater. Also, it has a north-bound current of up to 4 knots forming the Gulf Stream. This can push an east – or west-bound vessel miles off its intended course. As well, the area is subject to magnetic irregularities affecting compass readings. All this can lead to navigation problems that sailors were convinced were a result of mysterious behaviour. I don't believe it is.

November 15, 1979, we slipped out of the harbour, again. I was in the habit of checking the barometer daily. This morning it was at 30.1 inches, a comfortable reading. It was very cold but sunny; winds were light from the south-west, but unfortunately we were going against the Gulf Stream. Our distance travelled was discouragingly less than our indicated speed on the knot meter because of the current. During daylight, it was safe to come closer to shore where the Gulf Stream was minimal. In fact, we often got a counter current. At night we kept well offshore for safety reasons. The moon didn't appear until 0300 hours, so it was pitch black most of the night. We were now 3,500 miles from Whitby. Everyone had settled in and were less apprehensive this time around. At 1900 hours, we were still under motor and saw some strange orange lights north-west of us. Our chart indicated that we were in a Navy practice area, so we concluded that is what it was. The wind came up at 2100 hours, and we were thrilled to be under sail again. The tug *Adventure's* captain called me and thought we were on a collision course with him, but he must have been looking at someone else, as we were well clear of him when he came into view.

The next three days varied from being hove to in strong winds from the south to gentle winds that we could reach under full sail, and even a few hours under spinnaker. Finally, after five days, we fetched the entrance to Palm Beach at 1930 hours. It was pitch black. The entrance was very narrow, and it was extremely difficult to see because of all the blinding lights onshore from cars. We made about three passes before we finally gained enough courage to navigate the entrance. Once inside, the water was flat calm and crystal clear so we were happy to stay for four days. We socialized with friends on *Trillium*, *Reflection* and *Sauterelle* again, as we had left Beaufort just after them. It was like the tropics with the warm weather and crystal clear water. The kids found friends to hang out with, and we all felt it was worth the discomfort we had experienced getting this far. I did repair work on the boat, which took four hours to do an hour's work because of all of the visitors voicing their opinion on how it should be done. Finally, we were able to tear ourselves away and headed down the Gold Coast, the inland waterway to Fort Lauderdale. The shore was lined with beautiful homes. We anchored, dinghied ashore, walked downtown, and enjoyed a relaxing, fear-free day of not being on the ocean.

The next day, we motored into Bahia Mar Marina, still in Fort Lauderdale. Grand in wealth and appearance, our boat took on the appearance of a dinghy amongst all the huge luxurious yachts.

We gassed up, showered and departed late afternoon for our overnight sail across the Gulf Stream. We were on our way to the Virgin Islands, yet again. After clearing customs and immigration at Lucaya on Grand Bahama Island, we proceeded to Freeport before tackling the final leg to our destination. Lucaya had been devastated by hurricane David in 1979.

The following day we went into Freeport and ran into Real on *Bird*, who headed an expedition around the north-west Passage. We had met Andre, one of the crew members, in Tadoussac on a schooner. He was as surprised to see us again as we were to see him.

Now we were on our final leg. It was great to be back at sea. We had light winds, strong winds, big waves, small waves, lots of sail changes from reefed main and storm jib to spinnaker, full main and 180% genoa.

I took sights with my sextant daily, using the sun during the day and the stars at night, marking our longitude and latitude on our chart. It was 1,156 miles from Florida, which took eleven days. Not really a fast passage but a comfortable one. Once we were under seventy degrees longitude, we could start working our way south. It was encouraging to see our latitudes dwindle from twenty-six degrees down to twenty degrees. *We were getting closer!* Finally, at 0530, December 7, we could see lights on the horizon indicating we were dead on course.

Landfall! You can't imagine the elation we all felt. *We were finally here!* By 1600 hours, we had rounded the point and were in line with the narrow western entrance of the island of St. Thomas, leading into Charlotte Amalie. The engine wouldn't start, so we quickly inflated the dinghy, fitted the 4 hp outboard motor and started to tow *Melissa II* through the entrance. Sailing in was out of the question because of the wind turbulence created by the high mountains on either side. At the worst possible instant, the propeller blade came off the trusty 4 hp Evenrude. I immediately started rowing. We were drifting onto boats moored at Avery's Marina, but finally got an anchor down and dredged our way clear. *What an ending!* After clearing customs and immigration, Pat and our social butterflies were gallivanting around the marina making new friends while I stayed behind, working on the engine that was full of water. I had to take the oil pan off, remove the cylinder head and blow out the carburetor, soak everything in oil and put it all back together. It never did run very well after that, but with the trade winds blowing steadily out of the east, we seldom needed the engine.

We were so excited to finish the first phase of our journey. It was our intention to spend the winter months in the Caribbean then decide when we were going to go through the Panama Canal heading for Victoria. Well, as it turned out, we extended our travels multifold. We would cross the Atlantic and begin phase two of our adventure, but for now our winter stomping grounds were the Lesser Antilles from the Virgin Islands to Martinique.

About sixty miles east of Puerto Rico is St. Thomas, the most westerly of the US Virgin Islands (USVI). With the British Virgin Islands (BVI), they make up the finest cruising area in the world. From west to east, it is only thirty-five miles, with dozens of islands harboring spectacular snorkeling spots with crystal clear water. Because there are so many islands, you are protected from the heavy seas. The winds are constant; seldom exceeding 20 knots from the east. The major and largest US Virgin Island is St. Thomas, then St. John and St. Croix, and numerous small islands are within a few hours' sail.

To the east, the British Virgin Islands are made up of Tortola, Jost Van Dyke, and Virgin Gorda. Again there is a host of smaller islands a short sail away. The USVI and the BVI often conjure up images of pirates who roamed the area in the early 1700s, and so they should. Blackbeard, Captain Norman, Black Sam Bellamy, and William Kidd all found these islands a formable hiding place. Blackbeard's Castle stands high at Charlotte Amalie, although it is not clear whether he actually lived there. Piracy ran rampant in the years 1716 and 1726. The one who captured most of the folklore was Edward Teach, better known as Blackbeard. He got his comeuppance in 1718 in Beaufort, North Carolina, when he and many of his crew members were killed by British forces. Some of the smaller islands derived their name from the pirates: Norman Island and Dead Chest Island where Blackbeard abandoned some of his crew as punishment with only a machete and a bottle of rum for survival. Many tried to swim to nearby Peter Island, but most either drowned or were attacked by sharks.

After Columbus discovered the islands in 1493, over the next 200 years, they were held by many European powers, including Spain, Great Britain, the Netherlands, France, and Denmark-Norway. It wasn't until WWI that the US made a deal with Holland to establish the USVI. The British Virgin Islands came under British control in 1672 and became popular for sugar plantations. They survived on slavery for labour, so with the British abolition of slavery in 1834, sugar production declined. Charlotte Amalie became a major shipping port for goods exported to Europe. Today those same warehouses that were built to store goods are used for retail shops.

Lindbergh Bay is close to the St. Thomas airport. Whenever we had guests flying in for a visit, we would anchor there. Just around the corner to the east was the main harbour of Charlotte Amalie, where we established a bank account and received all our mail. The harbour often had over 900 boats at anchor with easy access to shore. It was also where the cruise ships came in, and on one occasion, there were eleven cruise ships in the harbour. Back in the early '80s one could board a cruise ship by carrying nothing more than a shopping bag and be taken for a passenger. I don't think that is the case today.

We seldom anchored in the harbour for more than a day or two but returned regularly for our mail and to get spending money. In fact, to avoid the hustle and bustle of Charlotte Amalie, we would go about seven miles east to Christmas Cove at Great St. James Island, our favourite snorkeling spot. It was surprising that we would often be the only vessel there when it is so close to St. Thomas . . . at least that was the case back then.

The next five months were gloriously spent exploring paradise. We experienced every anchorage in the Virgin Islands. Norman Island apparently inspired Robert Louis Stevenson's novel *Treasure Island*. The story goes that pirates hid treasure in the three caves off the west end of the island. The 400-foot mountaintop was used by pirates to scan the horizon in search of the feared British naval vessels. The Bight, a favourite anchorage for boaters, had a floating restaurant frequented by sharks looking for a free meal of leftovers. East of Norman Island is Peter Island with a beautiful beach on the south side facing Sir Francis Drake Channel, a great place to pick up coconuts that have fallen off the trees. Just east of it is Dead Chest Island then Salt Island, named after the salt pond, which was inhabited at the time by three families. Each year, they paid annual rent to the Queen of one pound of salt, which they collected from a large salt pond on the south side of the island. On our visit, Mrs. Clearance Smith greeted us and was most hospitable. She explained that the island is known for the wreck of the Royal Mail packet steamer RMS Rhone that sank in a hurricane on October 29, 1867, while trying to get out to sea. Most of the ship's crew was lost, and there are headstones along the shore to honour them.

To the north of this string of small islands is Tortola, meaning the land of the turtle dove, named by Columbus in 1493 when he discovered the Virgin Islands. It is the largest of the BVI, and the main town, Roadtown, is the capital. It is reported that Blackbeard and Captain Kidd lived there in the early 1700s. Of the many popular anchorages on Tortola, our favourite was Trellis Bay on Beef Island, which almost joins the main island. We stumbled onto a quaint restaurant, The Last Resort, owned and operated by Tony Snell and his wife Jackie. When I refer to it as quaint, it is because there was often a donkey that would stick his head through the window over our table while we were having dinner. Tony was a great performer and rewrote the lyrics to many songs. My favourite was, "You picked a fine time to heave up, Lucille" to the tune of, "You picked a fine time to leave me, Lucille." Years later, we chartered in the Virgin Islands and revisited The Last Resort. The donkey had become cantankerous and had to be kept in a stall built in the dining room. Yes, a stall in the dining room.

The girls had many friends

Play time after school

Still further to the east lay Virgin Gorda, where we often anchored to experience The Baths, a most unusual geological formation of granite boulders ten to thirty feet high resting on the beach. Some extend into the water forming large caves that you have to swim under water to enter. Jost Van Dyke lies about five miles north of St. John, although it is still part of the British Virgin Islands. There are some good anchorages there, but for us the big attraction was the Bubbly Pools, a short distant from Foxy's Taboo restaurant at Diamond Cay. This quiet pool about fifty feet in diameter flushes like a toilet every few minutes when a large wave filters in through narrow rocks separating it from the ocean. *It really is quite a thrill!*

About fifteen miles north of Virgin Gorda is the island of Anegada, which is made up of coral and limestone, unlike the other islands that are volcanic in origin. Because the approach from the south is very shallow and dangerous, it is not often visited by yachtsman. Denny Fricke flew me over it in his plane one day, and the bottom was crystal clear and spotted with large sharks. Thirty-five miles south from St. Thomas is another one of the seldom-visited Virgin Islands, St. Croix, and part of the USVI. Because it is due south and the trades are from the east, it was a pleasant speedy reach all the way there and back.

We went into the harbour of Christiansted, the capital, intending to anchor; however, we were chased away by some unfriendly yachtsmen, so we anchored in the outer harbour where it was uncomfortably rough. Pat and I dinghied into the main wharf to clear customs and waited for an hour and a half for a rude official who was annoyed that we didn't have the kids with us. We had left them on *Melissa II* because of the rough passage by dinghy. Had he insisted on us taking him out to the boat, he would have been drenched enroute.

We were very happy to leave early the next morning to go the short distance to Buck Island. There we enjoyed the underwater trail, snorkeling before going ashore to do some hiking. It turned out to be a good trip, and we were sure there were some wonderful people on St. Croix. *Alas, we just didn't happen to meet any of them.*

Upon our return to Red Hook on St. Thomas, we met the Barretts, whom we had last seen in Beaufort, North Carolina. It was a pleasant surprise. We had nicknamed Dave "Hurricane Dave" as he was the antithesis of the recent hurricane. He was very methodical and never in a hurry. When we dove for conch in thirty feet of water, he could scurry around the bottom and round up three conchs. I could only hold my breath long enough to pick up one. He proved to be a great travelling companion.

Our coconut supply in the BVIs

The Baths on Virgin Gorda, BVI

Conch cleaning

We danced to steel bands at the many Jump-ups, roamed the old sugar plantations that flourished back in the late 1700s, speared spiny lobster, dove for conch and picked fresh coconuts off the ground. We made lots of friends with other boaters who were doing the same thing we were; Julie and Jennifer had lots of kids to chum around with. It was amazing how quickly friendships formed with fellow boaters.

We did a lot of gunkholing, and one evening at Cruz Bay, USVI, we had seventeen people aboard *Melissa II,* our little twenty-nine-foot boat. Pat's mother flew in from Ottawa for a visit. We had arranged a hotel in Roadtown, BVI, but she was quite happy to cruise aboard the *Melissa II* for our day trips. One day we picnicked on Henley Cay, a wonderful place to snorkel. In fact, while snorkeling with Rod Forrester a few hundred feet offshore, we were shocked and indeed terrified to see a humpback whale with her calf breaching not 200 feet from us. With snorkels on we could actually see them underwater, which was quite a sight. Where else but the Virgin Islands would you be able to see 200 feet underwater?

CHAPTER 4

Be Yourself at Sea

Pat was inspired by the writing of Janice Ameen, a sixteen-year-old girl scout who sailed on the *Young America*. Here's a quote from her diary:

> "All of us encounter problems and worries during our life-
> time. Most of us worry about bills, work and making a living.
> We also worry about if we look nice enough to go out. We are
> all afraid of what others think of us, if they like us and if they
> will accept us. Sometimes we pretend to be what we aren't to
> please others. We also wonder where we are going in life, who
> we are as individuals, do we fit in? At sea there are no electric
> bills, phone bills or clothing bills to pay. There is no place to
> spend the money you have earned. There is no need to dress
> up for there is no one to impress. This has to be one of the
> greatest aspects of sailing. Society is miles away. At last you
> can be yourself and if you are not sure of what yourself is like,
> there is time to find out. Each sunrise and sunset takes on a
> special meaning. Sitting up in the crow's nest with ocean in
> every direction, you can feel the tranquility. There is time to
> just think about everything you have done and time to think
> about all the things you have left to do. There is no limit at
> sea. You can be you and not be doubtful and afraid. Being at
> sea offers you a sense of pride and accomplishment. Seeing
> the sails set and feeling the power of the wind moving the
> boat, you realize that you are a part of it all. You have hauled
> those lines until your hands sting and the result is the ship
> sailing through the water powered by nature. At sea I have

learned what teamwork is, what understanding is and how good it feels to like yourself and what you are doing. The ocean has so much to offer each one of us. You will never know what kind of person you are mentally, physically and emotionally until you go to sea."

CHAPTER 5
Explore the Lesser Antilles

"Hark, now hear the sailors cry, smell the sea, and feel the sky, let your soul and spirit fly, into the mystic and I shall watch the ferry boats, and they'll get high, on a bluer ocean against tomorrow's sky."

– Van Morrison

Off we went on a trip of 450 miles down the Lesser Antilles. We convinced the *Vargon* and *Nereid* crew to join us. On the windward side of the islands you are protected from the Atlantic swells but benefit from the trade winds. It is a reach all the way down and all the way back.

I was absorbed in the history and folklore of each island. We decided to go south as far as Martinique, an overseas region of France, then work our way back to the Virgin Islands, stopping at various islands. After sailing three days and nights, we made landfall in Fort-de-France, the capital of Martinique. We cleared customs and arranged to rent two CV4 Citroens and began to explore the island. Martinique was first discovered by Christopher Columbus. Although he was Italian, he received backing for his exploits from King Ferdinand and Queen Isabella of Spain. In 1493, on the second of his three voyages, he discovered and charted most of the Caribbean Islands. Spain wasn't that interested in Martinique, so it eventually became French.

We visited the town of Saint-Pierre, the former cultural centre of Martinique, referred to as the Paris of the Caribbean. In 1902, it suffered the devastating volcanic eruption of Mount Pelée, resulting in the death of 30,000 people. There were two survivors: one a criminal imprisoned underground in a cave; the other was the sole occupant of a ship in dock who immediately cast off the lines and cleared the harbour. As it turned out, the prisoner didn't do that badly. He joined Barnum and Bailey's Greatest Show on Earth. There was also a report of a young girl survivor who was found in a small boat a couple of miles offshore. At any rate, the town was completely obliterated, so we saw it in its rebuilt state. Further up the island, we visited the church where Joséphine was baptized in 1763. We marveled at the beauty of the island with banana, sugar cane, and pineapple plants along the roadside.

The next afternoon, we departed for Portsmouth, Dominique, known as the Nature Isle of the Caribbean for its natural beauty. Ester Williams starred in a movie filmed there in one of the splendid pools fed by a waterfall.

It was 1980, and Dominique hadn't recovered from Hurricane David, which had struck in 1979. It suffered more than the other islands of the Lesser Antilles. We entered the bay at Roseau, the capital and port of entry. *Vargon* and *Nereid* joined us. As we were anchoring, a group of teenagers in small rowboats descended on us, yelling and screaming that they would look after our boat and row us ashore. There were a dozen rowboats with one or two kids in each. We felt very uncomfortable, and it appeared that we had to hire three of them to take each of us ashore. While we were being rowed ashore, we could see the others hanging onto the gunnels of our boats at anchor. It appeared we had to hire them also to "look after our boats."

It didn't get better. We walked to the customs office and were admitted one group at a time while the others waited on the street. The streets were desolate and the buildings were in deplorable condition from the hurricane damage. There were fees but no receipts offered. Nervous about our boats, we hurried back and then decided to raft them together, keeping a constant watch throughout the night. Again the following morning, the kids appeared on the beach and were preparing to come out to us; however, we weighed anchor and hurriedly left, leaving them yelling disapproval of our departure, even though we had already given them money. Unfortunately, we didn't have the pleasure of taking in the beautiful sights of the island.

It was only twenty miles to our next anchorage, Îles des Saintes, a group of small islands spanning only seven miles. It is a favourite vacation spot for Guadeloupians who can fly there, landing on a small airstrip. At one end of the island, high on a mountain is Fort Napoléon; on the other end on a high mountain is Fort Joséphine.

Anchored in the bay, we met up again with our friends Nils and Chris aboard *Betelgeuse*. We had last met them in Beaufort. We walked the beach on the windward side and saw where Hurricane David had torn up a strip of paved road. After exploring the island, we all got together on *Neried* for dinner and a pleasant evening.

Our next anchorage was at La Chaise on the island of Guadeloupe. The three of us anchored in the harbour and socialized over dinner while we made plans for the next day.

The following morning, we cleared customs and took a bus to Pointe-à-Pitre, about twenty-five miles away past sugar cane fields, banana groves and picturesque little towns. We enjoyed touring the markets and had a *banqeets* for lunch, very tasty deep-fried bread with bits of chicken rolled up in it. On our return to the boats, we dined at a restaurant called Madam R. Racine's for a birthday celebration for "Hurricane David", our nickname for the skipper on *Vargon*. The food was good but outrageously expensive, so much so that we had to pay extra for the tap water and butter for our bread. We joked that the *R.* in Madam R. Racine stood for *Rip-off!*

Antigua was our next destination. Despite being only forty miles away, it was seven and a half hours of sailing with constant sail changes. We started in light east winds with a 180% genoa then, as the wind piped up, we changed to a 150, then 110, then a lapper and one reef in the main, eventually having to put another reef in the main. In spite of rough seas, we averaged 5.3 knots, arriving in English Harbour where we cleared customs and finally anchored. We were by far the smallest yacht there. Some had dinghies for reaching ashore that were larger than *Melissa II*. We watched one yacht lower a large wharf on davits in order to accommodate a dinghy and two Sea-Doos. We felt a little out of our element, but I enjoyed watching the nude girls parading on deck of some of these lavish yachts.

Columbus discovered Antigua in 1493. The island is best known for English Harbour, which offers great protection from tropical storms and is located at the south end adjacent to the town of Falmouth. In 1725, a dockyard was established to provide a base for British ships to patrol the West Indies and maintain Britain's sea power. It was later named after Horatio Nelson, the naval officer in charge in the late 1700s.

Just around the corner is Falmouth Bay. We were surprised to see Ric and Annette aboard *Sauterelle* at anchor. Eventually, *Vargon* joined us. We all gathered aboard *Sauterelle* where we had a catch-up over a feed of Lobster Thermidor prepared with lobster Ric had speared that day.

The next day we took a bus to St John's, which is the capital city of Antigua. A large majority of the wooden sailboats seen in the Lesser Antilles were built at the boatyard in St. John's. It was fascinating to see the naturally curved lumber forming the frames. The boats range up to forty feet long, and are used to deliver produce to the various islands. Because the winds are ninety degrees to the direction of travel, it is a reach which they do very well but into the wind they don't point efficiently.

After busing back to Falmouth, we hiked up to Shirley Heights Blockade. It is obvious why this was the location for a blockade, as there are panoramic views of English Bay, Falmouth Harbour, Nonsuch Bay, and the ocean beyond. Any approaching ships could be sighted early and signals sent down to Nelson's Dockyard to prepare to fend off. The original canons are still in place at the entrance of the bay. Upon our return, we departed for Marmora Bay, a comfortable anchorage just around the corner east of English Bay. David had made the decision to finish the trip on his own. We were going too quickly for his liking, so we said our goodbyes and arranged to get back together when we got home (the Virgin Island's home).

The route we had chosen to go from Antigua to Saint Maarten bypassed St. Kitts and Nevis to the west and St. Barts to the east. We averaged a creditable 6.25 knots for the 103-mile run to Philipsburg, St. Maarten. The southern half of St. Maarten is Dutch, with Dutch as the official language. The northern half is French, and the official language is French. The story goes that a Frenchman was taken ashore on the north coast and a Dutchman on the south coast. They walked until they met each other, which determined the border between the Dutch and the French. The island is only eight miles from north to south. We spent a day of walking the streets of Philipsburg before taking a bus to the French half at Margot Bay.

It was time to head home to the Virgin Islands. We cleared customs and got under way about 1300 hours and caught an amber jack just out of the anchorage. According to our fish book, it was second only to large barracuda for ciguatera poisoning, which can be fatal. It is caused by eating certain reef fish whose flesh is contaminated with toxins in tropical and subtropical waters that in turn are eaten by larger carnivorous fish. We didn't want to take any chances, so we didn't eat the jack. We had light winds from the north-east through the night until we fetched Cruz Bay, USVI, at 0800 hours. We cleared customs and headed for Red Hook, on St. Thomas, to take on fuel. When we arrived, we had a great reunion with the Foresters aboard *Nous Deux*.

CHAPTER 6

Home Again in the Virgin Islands

"If it's brown go around, if it's green it's lean, if it's blue go through."

– Pamela

We arrived back feeling that we were home again. At this point, it didn't seem like a vacation but rather a way of life in a small community but with boats, not houses. We could be by ourselves if we chose, or we could go on little adventures with friends. I guess you would have to say it was a bit like a vacation because we didn't have to go to work next day. The girls actually enjoyed doing their school work, and for us it was wonderful to see their commitment without any parental guidance. They did school work in the mornings, then socialized with their friends in the afternoon and evening. We enjoyed having family and friends visiting us. In fact, one time we sailed out to meet a cruise ship that was coming into the Charlotte Amalie harbour. The ship called us on the radio to inform us that a good friend of ours Jim Preston, was on board and they requested permission to lower him down on a sling to board our boat. This took place about three miles out from the harbour. It was quite a procedure under the watchful eyes of hundreds of passengers. We took him to Christmas Cove for a day of snorkeling before he taxied to the dock to re-embark. He was faced with a deluge of questions about his experience by fellow passengers. It is unlikely a cruise ship would do that today.

For the next month, we visited our old haunts. We dove the caves at Norman Island, swam The Baths and took in the steel band playing at Caneel Bay. Located on the western end of the island of St. John, it was a favourite of ours. The resort, which formed part of the Virgin Island National Park, was originally owned by Laurence Rockefeller. He was so taken by the beauty of St. John that he purchased most of the island, and then donated a big portion to the US government for the park, which wasn't a bad idea because the government looked after all the maintenance. The resort, which featured a tremendous steel band on the weekends, had no objection to us boaters coming ashore by dinghy to enjoy the music. I was told that they welcomed it as it contributed to the ambiance for their guests to enjoy.

While going to the various locations in the USVI, we were required to clear customs. When we checked in at Cruise Bay on St. John, we were told we could get a cruising permit, removing the necessity to clear customs at every landfall. I wondered why we hadn't been told that four months earlier.

We went to Christmas Cove to meet friends aboard *Circe*. They asked us to crew for them for the S.T.Y.C. Rolex Regatta aboard his Sparkman & Stevens 37. After the race, we enjoyed the festivities at the yacht club, just a dinghy ride across from Christmas Cove.

Before Pat and I discussed where we would go from here, I had to clean the bottom, which had become a bit of a ritual when at Christmas Cove. I was always accompanied by a four-foot barracuda, the same one I'm sure. When I finished one side, he would follow me over to the other side. Colourful small fish would feed on what I scraped off, but he would stand off about six or eight feet and just watch. I wish I could have petted him, but when I approached he would back away. I named him "Barry the Barracuda."

We had been in the Caribbean for almost four months now. We realized it was not a good idea to stay the summer. The heat was extreme, but it was hurricane season and could be risky for our boat. It appeared that I had to clear up some legal matters with my ex-business partners in Toronto, which would entail going back. We could put *Melissa II* up on the hard and fly back. We were considering something else as well. Robert Louis Stevenson said he travelled not to go anywhere but just to go. John Steinbeck said for him it was "the urge to be someplace else", something I could identify with both of them. A sailboat was the cheapest way to get to where we wanted to go. *How about crossing the Atlantic to England?* We were heading back to Victoria, but we were not in any hurry to get there. The kids' school work was going really well, so there was little urgency to return.

We finally decided that we would sail back to Beaufort, North Carolina. We would leave the *Melissa II* there and bus back to Ontario, take care of business and visit friends for the summer, and then take the bus back to the boat and cross the Atlantic.

We contacted our friends, who were looking after all our financial affairs. *There was no Internet in those days!* They were fruit farmers in Vineland, the Niagara Peninsula. Craig suggested he could put me to work at the farm for the summer and could provide a derelict old house on a piece of property he had recently purchased. He was going to tear it down, but it would be adequate for us to camp in. After all, we were used to living on a twenty-nine-foot boat.

Sailing back to Beaufort would be quite an adventure in itself—and it was. We departed Christmas Cove at 0630 on April 7, exactly four months from the day we arrived in the Virgin Islands. Our first landfall was Samana, Dominican Republic, a three-day sail of 267 miles. Wind was typically behind when heading west. It was a comfortable sail through the nights. Being close enough to shore, we could make out landmarks for dead reckoning and didn't have to rely on astronomical observations. We flew the yellow quarantine flag and were almost immediately boarded by three very courteous officials to give us clearance. Samana had suffered a hurricane a few years previously and was in the process of rebuilding. It looked pretty desperate. It appeared that crime was a problem, and the streets were lined with the military carrying machine guns.

We had a four-day layover while waiting for *Naried* and *Nous Deux* to arrive, as we had agreed to wait for them to sail onto Puerto Plata to do some sightseeing. After their arrival the following day, we departed fighting head seas and head-winds going east to get around Cabo Samana for five miles before we rounded the cape and headed west through the night, reaching the entrance to Puerto Plata at 0400. It was dark and looked risky, so we hove to back-winding our sails for three hours before heading in the harbour. Again they were very courteous and cleared us but took our rifle, giving us a receipt. On the advice of offshore sailors, we had acquired a Winchester 30-30 hunting rifle in Beaufort, NC. They had convinced me that, travelling with three girls, a weapon on board would be a good idea; however, it always proved to be a problem clearing customs in foreign countries.

The docking facilities offered free electricity, water and showers, but we chose to anchor in the harbour. It just made us feel more comfortable. On his first voyage, Christopher Columbus observed that the mountain that is within the city was usually shrouded in silvery cloud and therefore called it the silver port, Puerto Plata. A tramway, which is almost 800 feet high, leads up the mountain to a botanical garden and a huge statue of Christ. It was only operational when cruise ships were in port, so we were unable to go. The downtown market was bustling with activity, which was hardly surprising given the bargains that were available.

We taxied to Santo Domingo on the south shore of the Dominican Republic and saw a statue of Christopher Columbus. On our taxi ride across the width of the island, we saw people were living in lean-tos made of corrugated sheet metal, salvaged after World War II. Poverty was evident everywhere except when entering Santo Domingo, where we saw a huge mansion guarded by armed police or military, all carrying assault weapons. We assumed it was the governor or some high-ranking official. Traffic included pedestrians, people on horses or bicycles and very few cars, but we did see a small two-door Toyota with nine people in or on it, which made us feel humble and was quite an example for our kids to witness.

We didn't weigh anchor until 1530 hours because we wanted to arrive at the Turks and Caicos in the morning. After saying our goodbyes to our friends that were staying behind, we made better time than anticipated. We were abeam of Bush Cay by 0600 hours. It was a comfortable reach the whole way but we were driven twelve miles west by the current. The approach of fifty miles or so is extremely shallow and includes reefs on the east and west side of Turk Island Passage. The Turks and Caicos are about sixty miles from one end to the other and about ten miles wide. It is believed that the first inhabitants of the islands crossed over from Hispaniola sometime from 500 to 800 AD. The Spanish captured the island inhabitants and enslaved them in the early 1500s. During the following 300 years, its control went from the Spanish, the French and finally to the British. On three occasions, Canada looked at acquiring the Turks and Caicos, but it never came to fruition.

I didn't get to see much of the low-lying Turks and Caicos. While Pat went ashore at Cockburn to clear customs, I took the cylinder head off the engine, cleaned points, carburetor and distributor, only to discover there was zero compression on cylinders 1, 2, and 4. Not good on a four-cylinder engine. It wouldn't start, but we were a sailboat after all, so we sailed out of the anchorage bound for the Bahamas. When I pulled up the anchor at 0730, I noticed a huge triton shell lying on the bottom. I dove to bring it on board, but not being able to get the critter out, it sat on the deck stinking for a year before it became a keepsake.

Sailing for the north side of the island, we lost and caught lots of fish, including a twenty-pound horse-eye jack, which we threw back. One of the lost fish was a huge Dorado (dolphin fish, mahi mahi) that we would have loved to eat for dinner. We had to settle for a couple of two-pound jacks, which were very good the way Pat cooked them. Although intending to anchor overnight at the north end of the island, we were faced with a very narrow, shallow passage with breaking water to the anchorage. I considered inflating the dinghy and marking a safe channel with rubber fenders guiding us to the anchorage. Finally I decided against it as it was too risky. We decided to carry on to Mayaguana Island, the most south-easterly end of the Bahamas, a comfortable sail with the wind steady on the port quarter, with the main and the 150 genoa. By 0530, we spotted a ship at the east end of Mayaguana shoal, but it turned out to be a wreck, although it looked to be intact and wasn't listing. After twenty-three hours, we had covered 110 miles.

It was back to engine repairs with hopes of at least getting it to plug along. The kids did school work, while Pat did cleanup with me in her way. We were in for quite a night. It started with lightning and thunder, and then the wind increased to 30 knots. We were being set on a lee shore. The waves grew bigger and were braking. *Sleep was out of the question!* We were dragging anchor. I inflated the dinghy and set the stern anchor, as well as letting out more scope on the main anchor. Poor Jennifer was sick to her stomach and crying uncontrollably. I tied our 1,000 feet to the stern of *Melissa II*, got in the dinghy with her and fed the line to shore. This left Pat on the boat terrified, watching the waves breaking and driving us closer to shore.

I chatted with Jennifer and eventually calmed her down as we walked back and forth along the beach. In fact, we picked up a glass ball and some shells that pleased her. Seeing her mom was troubled, she agreed to go back to the boat. We got in the dinghy and pulled on the line to get us back to *Melissa II* through the breakers. I was yelling to Pat that I was going to take the stern anchor with our 1,000 feet of yacht braid out to windward and set it. The plan was to cautiously winch up the main anchor then tack back and forth with a reefed main and storm jib against the breaking waves until we were clear of them, which we did.

We sailed over the stern anchor, and I secured a float on the line so it could be retrieved. This turned out to be an all-day job.

By 1600 hours, the wind had died down. The swells were still broad-siding us, but we were safe! Pat had spent a lot of time in the boat by herself under dreadful conditions. She preferred to leave me in the boat with the kids while she retrieved the anchor, which meant rowing the dinghy to the anchor float, reeling in the 1,000 feet of line, pulling up the anchor and rowing back to *Melissa II*. Despite having endured an unnerving experience, we jumped up and down for joy for what we had accomplished. If our engine had been working, we could have just motored our way to safety. Our little 4 hp dinghy motor was completely useless against the breaking waves, which was why we had to relying on rowing.

Our destination was Georgetown, the capital of the Exumas, with a population of about 800, and quite likely the best place en route to get the parts to repair my engine. It took six days to cover less than 200 miles. If we had had a motor, it would have taken us a day and a half. Since the winds were virtually nonexistent, we often drifted for six hours at a time. When we did pick up some wind, it was so light that we hardly had enough for steerage. We had rain squalls, and thunder and lightning. And while the kids were content to push ahead with school work, Pat and I just sat in the cockpit, carrying out our watches night and day, wondering why on Earth we were doing this.

There were some pleasant moments. One morning, we saw a number of huge dolphin fish (mahi mahi, dorado) swimming around our boat. They were so colourful. We had never seen dolphin fish other than on the end of a hook. I had never heard that they could be in schools; especially such large ones. Some must have weighed twenty pounds. We were so exhausted; we didn't even consider trying to catch one. After six days of this, we finally were abeam of the entrance to Georgetown. It was 2300 hours with no wind and it was very dark. We inflated the dinghy, attached the 4 hp Evenrude outboard and tried to push *Melissa II* through the narrow entrance, but gave up because it just looked too risky. Having had enough excitement, we dropped anchor and waited it out until morning, when we tried again. Fortunately, a Morgan 42 (sailboat) was entering the harbour just at that time and could see the difficulty we were in and kindly towed us to the anchorage. We went in to clear custom and found the town was in chaos. We had arrived during the Island Family Regatta, cleared customs, picked up some money at the local bank and returned to the anchorage. We were amazed to discover that we knew most of the boats.

For the next fifteen days, we experienced no end of frustration. Using the boomvang, I hoisted the engine onto the cabin sole in the main living area (much to Pat's delight), then disassembled it, discovering that three exhaust valves had to be replaced.

Engine repairs

After I took them to the local garage, the owner's brother was going to take them to Nassau to have them resurfaced and returned the following day. However, by Thursday there were still no valves, so I phoned a garage in Miami, Florida. The phone call cost $4.50, and the mechanic I spoke to had never heard of an Atomic 4 engine, one of the most popular engines used on cruisers under forty-feet in those days. He suggested I call a distributor also in Miami, which I did from the same phone booth ($9.00). He had them, but he had to have the money first. I went to the Bank of Nova Scotia and asked them to send him the money. They said they could, but it would take a week. Back to the phone booth to call ($4.50) the distributor, who wasn't the least bit sympathetic. I called ($4.50) another marine garage in Fort Lauderdale, Florida, who took Chargex (now called VISA). The cost for the valves – not counting the phone calls – was $28.50 plus tax and air freight for a total of $66.91, maybe. This was 1980 remember. I borrowed a bicycle from one of the boaters and peddled three miles to the airport to meet the scheduled flight. *No valves!* At 0900 hours the next morning, I called ($4.50) the mechanic, who wasn't in at that time but I was told he would call me when he arrived. I waited by the phone booth until 1530 hours; no phone call.

I went back to the boat very discouraged. I lapped in the intake valves, making ready to complete the engine work once the valves arrived. I took both batteries to the dockside where Simonette, the mechanic, was going to pick them up, take them to the garage and put them on charge overnight. The next morning, they were at the dockside, and it became apparent that they hadn't been picked up yet. Simonette agreed to pick them up again and put them on charge. The following morning, he claimed he had misplaced them but searched while I was there and found them. I saw him put one on charge. Meantime, Pat took a package of the kids' school work and a few letters to friends and family to the post office. It was out of stamps! They said stamps were on their way from Nassau. It was exactly one week before they arrived. In the meantime, one battery did get charged, so that was going to be enough.

During that week, I made many trips to the airport and made many phone calls. Pat was afraid that I was going to tear the wings off the airplane if I went again so she offered to go. At 1030 hours, Pat arrived with the valves at a total cost of $156.91, not counting phone calls. I was ready. Simonette was out of lapping compound, so I used toothpaste to lap in the valves. At 1430 hours – some four hours later – we started the engine, weighed anchor and motored out of the harbour. We had been in Georgetown for fifteen days. At the sound of my motor starting, everyone came out on deck waving, blasting horns, and yelling *bon voyage*. We were on our way!

The Bahamas, officially the Commonwealth of The Bahamas, is one of only two countries whose official name begins with 'The'; the other one being The Gambia. It was Columbus's first landfall of the new world in 1492. In the early 1700s, it was a haven for pirates and became a British crown colony governed by Woodes Rogers. He suppressed the piracy problem by granting them immunity as long as they didn't pillage British ships. In other words, they could act as British warships. They could continue plundering Spanish ships or any other country's ships. It was very successful, and he quickly gained the support of the pirates. The Bahamas are in the North Atlantic and not in the Caribbean, as many people think. They cover 450 miles from south to north, whereas the Virgin Islands are only thirty-five miles east to west. It is a wonderful cruising ground for yachtsmen. Nassau is the capital. We were hightailing it back to North Carolina so we didn't have the time to do any gunkholing. Our long unscheduled stay in George Town fixed that. At that point, we didn't know what lay ahead, other than we had to get back to Ontario for the summer.

The trip to Morehead City near Beaufort was 870 miles, which we did nonstop. By and large, it was a fast trip. Weather-wise, we experienced everything from fearsome lightning storm to flat calm. Day after day, porpoises would accompany us. We lived on fresh fish for the whole journey; one Cero mackerel fed us for two days, which was boney, but tasted delicious. Our next catch was a dorado, a favourite of ours, and then while on a spinnaker run with Julie at the helm, she caught a fifty – pound Allison or yellowfin tuna. Getting it into the boat was quite an ordeal. I tried everything and ended up sticking my hand down its throat and grabbing his tail to hoist it onto the boat. It tasted like veal and lasted the rest of the trip. I'm sorry to say that we had to discard more than half of it but was happy that we were feeding other fish and crabs. Meanwhile, as we continued on our journey, we sat in the cockpit, talking of greater passages to England and beyond.

Tuna

Porpoise

A dorado, dolphin fish or mahi mahi as they are called in the Pacific.

Six large grey porpoises welcomed us and led us into the Morehead City, just a short distance from Beaufort. Our trip took us a little over five days for an average speed of 6.93 knots. The boost from the Gulf Stream was at times 4 knots. I took sun shots to verify our dead-reckoning position, and we were always farther along than we had plotted.

Once in the harbour, we cleared customs and made arrangements to moor the boat for the summer. Then it was packing, saying goodbye to all our Beaufort friends and hopping on a bus for Vineland near Toronto, Ontario, to begin my summer of farming. It was May 15, 1980.

We had a great summer! Pat, being a nurse, had no difficulty getting work at a nearby hospital. I was busy with a number of chores like delivering strawberries, peaches, apricots, and cherries by truck to various grocery stores in Toronto, as well as to the local distributor. Each Saturday, I would take a load of fresh fruit to the Kitchener market. Julie picked cherries and had a wonderful time with new friends in the Gillespie's swimming pool, as did Jennifer. Toronto was only a half-hour's drive away, so from time to time I would go there to look after legal affairs and visit friends. We arranged for Julie and Jennifer to meet their teacher, which was a real thrill for them, as they had been corresponding for a year. They were both doing really well and considered their teacher to be a close friend. We were very lucky that they enjoyed their studies so much.

The summer went by very quickly. I arranged to deliver a car to Florida from Toronto. I dropped Pat and the kids off at Morehead City then continued on my own to deliver the car and fly back from Florida.

CHAPTER 7
Winter in the Bahamas

"Twenty years from now you will be more disappointed by the things you didn't do than by the ones you did do. So throw off the bowlines. Sail away from safe harbour. Catch the trade winds in your sails. Explore. Dream. Discover."

– Mark Twain

It was November 13 when we arrived back at Morehead City. On our to-do list, there were numerous chores to be completed. Somehow, somewhere, we wanted to get a new diesel engine to replace our gasoline Atomic 4 engine that had caused us so much grief. Also, we wanted to replace our little Avon inflatable dinghy and the 4 hp engine with something larger. I had to pass my ham radio license and do a shakedown cruise to the Bahamas for the winter.

After studying a host of engines that would be suitable, we decided on a Yanmar 2GM, a two-cylinder, 15 hp diesel engine, and one hundred pounds lighter than the Atomic 4. The North American distributor I contacted told me that all of them were being disseminated to yacht builders. They did give me a contact list of the builders, as the next step was to see if I could convince one that it would be a good idea to sell me an engine. On the list was San Juan Yachts, builder of the San Juan 24, an I.O.R. quarter-ton racing boat that I knew from races against it in my Swiftsure 24, the original *Melissa*. Bruce Kirby, the designer of the San Juan 24, and his wife, Margo, used to live next door to my sister in Point Claire, Quebec, just west of Montreal so I was hopeful that that would give me some preferential status. I called San Juan Yachts, telling them my close connection with the world-famous designer and that my wife and my two little girls were stuck in North Carolina without an engine. After more begging and pleading, they finally agreed to ship one to me immediately.

It arrived and so the work began! I used the boomvang to hoist out our Atomic 4, leaving it on the dock with a sign, 'free'. After lowering the Yanmar into place, I discovered that the output shaft was three inches higher than the prop shaft. My six years of racing sports cars taught me that there are no mechanical problems, only solutions. Off I went to an automotive parts store to purchase two simple universal joints, a pillow block and a thrust bearing. I also had to fabricate motor mounts to accommodate the new motor. *It worked!* I never had to align the prop shaft again, as the universal joints took care of any alignment discrepancy. The only comment from the local marine mechanic was, "Don't be crazy. It will never work." I thought I had uncovered new ground but heard that motorboats often use universal joints. It turned out to be a little more complicated, as the clutch slipped. I discovered that the clutch relied on pressure from the prop shaft to engage it; however, the pillow block was not allowing the pressure to reach it, so I finally modified the clutch mechanism after no end of frustration and tinkering.

Next on the list was obtaining a larger inflatable dinghy. It just so happened that a local marine supply store was going out of business. That kind of news travels fast amongst the boating community. We purchased an eleven-foot Hutchinson inflatable that had a removable wooden floor, inflatable seat and a plastic windshield. A 15 HP Evinrude outboard motor was our next purchase, which was just perfect for the Hutchinson. All we had to do was find a place to store it on our overcrowded twenty-nine-foot sailboat. We already had a life raft stowed behind the mast. Deflated, it fit behind the life raft. To store it inflated, I scrounged some lengths of one-inch stainless steel tubing that I taped together to form collapsible davits, and then had it welded together at a local welding shop. While in anchorages or travelling short distances in calm water, it was perfect. The davits folded out of the way against the stern when not in use.

We planned to have a shakedown cruise to the Bahamas for the winter and departed early morning in the dark for Whitesville, NC. Going against the Gulf Stream, we had to stay close to shore to avoid the strong current against us. We had experienced this on our previous trip to Florida. We reached Whitesville late in the day and, as expected, it was dark, and then began a comedy of errors that didn't seem that funny at the time. First, while approaching the dock to call customs with Pat at the helm, the shift lever came off, and we were stuck in reverse. There was no space at the dock, so we were going to anchor seeking it in reverse. The depth-sounder packed up, so I inflated the dinghy and, with a long line, sounded the bay for a safe place to anchor. Once we had decided on a spot, I scurried aboard to let out the anchor. The chain jammed in the hawser. I fetched the stern anchor and brought it forward finally and got us squared away; all of this in the dark. *Who said sailing isn't fun!* We finally settled down to eating chocolate squares and enjoying a good laugh.

From Wrightsville, we carried on down the coast, seeing lots of sandy beaches with little fishing villages at each inlet. We saw many commercial fishing boats but little else. After we passed Georgetown, SC, it appeared quite marshy. We pulled alongside an outboard-driven skiff and bought a shad to have for dinner. It was a really tasty male. We were told that the female shad were more expensive because of the roe. When we passed the Cape Fear River inlet, we got quite a boost from the current pushing us south-west along the coast of South Carolina. We were still having transmission problems, so when we got to Charleston, I contacted "John, John the Yanmar man", who agreed to meet us at the dock. He discovered a weak spring in the clutch mechanism and replaced it. Also one of the motor mounts appeared loose, so I fiber glassed it in place. During our layover in Charleston, we shopped, did laundry, did lots of sightseeing and generally spent evenings gamming with the other yachtsmen.

Sailing down the coast to West Palm Beach, we had to stay close to shore to avoid the Gulf Stream going against us, in some places up to 4 knots. We had done this before. Being so close to shore day and night was really nerve-racking. By midnight, we were at the entrance of West Palm Beach, which offered a challenge to work our way into. It wasn't something we hadn't done before, but what a relief when we finally dropped anchor. From here to Fort Lauderdale, we would be going down the Gold Coast, so called for its constant display of wealth. The homes were gorgeous and it is certainly not a lifestyle that we had experienced. After eventually reaching Miami at 2300 hours, we listened to the weather report and decided to depart for Bimini – "The gateway to the Bahamas" – at midnight. That way we would cross the Gulf Stream at night, arriving to clear customs in the morning. The Gulf Stream had set us north ten miles during the night, so we had to sail south to get to Bimini. As we approached the harbour, three maxi boats crossed our bow: *Mistress Quickly* from Australia,

Jupiter and *Humblebee*. It is likely they were returning home from the Bermuda-Nassau race. *What a sight!*

I threw out a fishing line, and before it was out a boat length, we hooked an eight-pound dorado, which we enjoyed for dinner that evening. Our mode of fishing was to trail a 200-pound nylon test line behind the boat with a giant hook tied to the end and wrapped with bright-coloured spinnaker cloth, which we had on board for repairs and for fabricating courtesy flags for the various countries we visited.

Pat fabricating a courteously flag

After a long wait to clear customs, we sailed over to Gun Cay for the night. The water was crystal clear, and there was lots of conch, but I didn't bother diving for them. Had there been lobster, I would have been diving with my Hawaiian sling. I spent the following day making ratlines until 1800 hours. It took twenty-four splices, with a whip at each end, so was very time-consuming.

The girls spent their day tidying up and reorganizing lockers. We were getting geared up for our winter in the Bahamas.

There are twenty-nine islands in the Bahamas. Well, maybe 3,000, but most are a chain of islands strung out from one of the major ones. We lived on conch fritters, lobster, grouper, and grunts . . . all caught ourselves by spear fishing. There was lots of socializing in the anchorages. One evening, a sailor yelled over at us: "Y'all come over for some grits and grunts." Grits are a favored Southern States dish made from corn; grunts are a white fish that are common in tropical waters. *We did and they were great!*

We met boats in the anchorages that we had met before in Beaufort, NC, as well as one we recognized from the Virgin Islands. At Little Whale Cay, Larry Darnell aboard *Eden* came in to anchor. It was a howling wind; he was alone so I dinghied over to give him a hand. Larry was a professional diver who had taken an early retirement and had lots of shark stories to tell. We cruised with him for five days and had a wonderful time snorkeling, fishing, and doing boat repairs. The kids had lots of playtime scooting around in the dinghy and hanging out with their new friends. When it was mealtime, I would summons them by blowing on a conch shell that I kept on board for that purpose.

We found we were spending a lot of time cleaning the bottom, repairing sails, plugging leaks, and generally repairing gear . . . all very important because everything had to be shipshape for our Atlantic crossing.

Eventually, we headed for Nassau, the capital of the Bahamas, where we picked up our Vineland friends, Craig, Joyce, and their two children, with whom we had spent the summer. We had arranged accommodation for them at Staniel Cay, in the Exumas. But before arriving, we spent three days gunkholing, with all eight of us sleeping on the *Melissa II*, either on the floor, on deck or in the cockpit. One night at anchor we experienced horrendous 40-knot winds, which meant Craig and I had to keep watch overnight. With my Hawaiian sling – which is very much like a slingshot using a spear instead of a rock – we speared lobster, had lots of conch fritters, speared grouper and grunts. Craig was excited to catch a forty-eight-inch barracuda but disappointed that we couldn't eat it because of the possibility of ciguatera poisoning. The Gillespie family became so accustomed to the crowded living conditions on the boat that they convinced us to cancel their reservation at Staniel Cay. With so much going on from first thing in the morning until bedtime, they didn't want to miss anything.

Each day would start with the eight of us piling into the inflatable and heading off over the Great Bahama Bank. There was never a dull moment. The Banks are very shallow (seldom over six feet deep), which is ideal for swimming, snorkeling, and fishing. Every night, dinner was what we had caught that day, including red hind and Coney (both members of the grouper family), conch, and lobster. Can you imagine anyone saying: "Oh no! Not lobster again tonight?"

The two-week visit went very quickly. Half the time we anchored at Staniel Cay; the other half, we were gunkholing our way to Nassau. We past Norman Cay, where there was the headquarters for a Columbian illegal drug operation. Their leader, Carlos Lehder, was arrested in 1982. We could see the airstrip that accommodated the planes flying in from Columbia and armed guards watching over the dock. *We gave it a wide berth!*

We anchored at Allen Cay to view the rock iguanas. By today's standards, they are considered an endangered subspecies, but in 1981, we were not aware of it. Hordes of them would charge us, while undoubtedly looking for food, their vision is not very good, so they would run into our legs. Some were longer than four feet, head to tail. They would get into fights with each other, but they certainly didn't appear as a threat to us. I even attempted to pick one up, but it would have none of it, and just wiggled away.

the rock iguanas Allen Cay

One day, Craig and I took off in the dinghy to do some snorkeling near a coral reef, about a mile from the anchorage. Two or three hundred feet from the reef, we anchored, donned our fins and snorkels, and jumped in. Just as we reached the reef and were about to separate, with Craig going on one side and me on the other, I spotted a nurse shark. Of all the sharks, the nurse shark is the most docile, most of the time. I signaled to Craig to join me and pointed it out. It was only about fifty feet away but immediately sped towards us. Craig jumped out onto the reef, scraping his legs and arms quite severely. I waited until it was about two feet away before I jumped out too.

It was between six and eight feet long and probably would have just nudged me with his nose to see if I was worth eating. The problem that faced us both was that we were bleeding and somehow we had to get back to the dinghy. Although we couldn't see the shark, I was reluctant to jump in and start swimming so we stood on the reef, which was only about one hundred square feet, and started waving and yelling. We could see *Melissa II* and two other boats at the anchorage off in the distance, but none were paying any attention to us. In fact, we even doubted that they could see or hear us but were sure that, after a time, the girls would assume something was wrong and come to the rescue.

After an hour or so, we noticed a small dinghy leaving one of the boats, and heading out toward us. It got a little ways out and then turned back. It was likely that he had spotted our dinghy and assumed all we had to do was swim to it, so we started to wave and yell until we got his attention, and he altered his course toward us. His little inflatable only had a 2 hp motor, so it took some time for him to reach us. Paul – on *Foxy Lady*, an Ericson 39 – was our hero. I jumped into his dinghy, and he took me over to mine so I could pick up Craig and tow Paul back to his boat in the anchorage. Of course, when we reached *Melissa II*, the girls were there and asked: "Did you have fun?" We said "Well, we were almost eaten by a vicious shark, but other than that, Yes!"

We departed for Nassau at 0730 with two other boats, a forty-five-foot ketch and thirty-three-footer. Of course, *it was a race!* When do sailboats leave an anchorage and not race? It was a perfect 18 knot wind from ENE. Under full main and 130% genoa, we sailed into Nassau harbour, beating the other two boats. We covered the thirty-four miles in five hours twenty-five minutes, for an average speed of 6.48 knots, not that I was keeping track. This was going to be our last day together. *How sad!* We went out for dinner at the Harbour Cove Hotel, spending the evening rehashing our experiences over the last two weeks.

We had all enjoyed a wonderful time together, so when they boarded a taxi for the airport the next morning, we all had tears in our eyes. When we finally returned to the boat, the girls got on with their school work, I studied my ham radio course, and Pat organized our food locker and generally tidied things up. We went into the dock to gas up and fill our water tanks and we heard that a cigarette boat had left a week ago for Miami and hadn't been heard from. The big suspicion was that its disappearance was drug related. We never heard anything more. .

Because strong winds were predicted for the night, we anchored in the harbour, postponing our departure until the next day. We set out all our ground tackle in preparation for a windy night. We also arranged night watches, as the harbour was crowded. Sure enough, in the middle of the night, a boat was dragging anchor towards some other boats. We honked our horn to alert the skipper. A man and wife and their children were on board.

The boat was not in very good repair. The man was quite sleepy when he came out on deck, and when I yelled that he was dragging anchor, he insisted that it was me that was dragging anchor. He was obviously out of it because we wouldn't have been dragging and moving forward relative to him. Other skippers who were in the line of being rammed came out and assured him it was his anchor that was dragging. We later heard when we were back in Beaufort that when he was sailing in the Gulf Stream, his wife had fallen overboard. Apparently she was in the habit of sitting on the guardrail to urinate, and as a result, it was suspected that she fell overboard. Of course, there had to be a police investigation. It was very sad. When we arrived a month later in Beaufort, the boat was anchored there.

We departed late afternoon at 1830 hours with promises of light winds from the south-east. It turned out to be moderate winds of 20 knots from the north-east, the direction we were headed.

My log book reads: "Close hauled all night, into mountainous seas. One filled the cockpit and spilled down below, drenching our bedding, clothing, and upholstery."

We altered course to the Bight of the Abaco, fetching Sandy Point, at 0600 hours when it was still dark. We hove to for half an hour before visibility was good enough to safely enter the anchorage. When I started the engine, the buzzer warning light stayed on indicating overheating. My thought was that the dashboard had been drenched in saltwater and the electrics shorted out. It was terrible holding ground for the anchor. Pat and Jennifer went into town to shop while Julie and I dove to set the anchor, and then dealt with the electrics problem.

Sandy Point's main industry is conch and lobster that is shipped to mainland USA. The people are friendly, and the town is very clean. We took on water at the government wharf and readied ourselves for departure to Gorda Cay, which was only fifteen miles away. According to the chart, this small island looked like a pleasant safe anchorage. We were in for a bit of a surprise. Expecting it to be uninhabited, we were astonished to see four vicious guard dogs roaming the beach. There was a small cabin that didn't look much larger than a garage, but we didn't see anybody.

Pat and I left the girls to do school work while we went off in the dinghy to spear dinner. The usual procedure was for me to don my snorkel gear, hang my head over the side looking for fish, while Pat motored slowly along until I signalled to stop. The water was about thirty feet deep. All of a sudden, straight below us I saw a thirty-foot sloop resting on its side. It looked like it had run aground and sunk; the waves were washing it back into deeper water. The hatch was open, and upholstery and the boat's contents were floating around with the waves. It looked like it had happened recently. I didn't dive because I had just seen a lemon shark swimming under the dinghy.

We rushed back to *Melissa II* and had barely boarded when a plane came into view and landed on the island on what appeared to be a small airstrip. Now we were getting worried, so we all scurried down below and watched out the porthole with binoculars. We could see two men who got into a dinghy and headed out toward our boat. It turned out that they were hired to look after the island as the owner was planning to build a marina and resort. They were pleasant enough and informed us that the Bahamian government was being difficult by not granting them a permit unless they occupied the island for two years. Further to that, if the authorities found the island vacant, they would lose the opportunity to get the permit. They invited us to shore for refreshments and to see architectural drawings of Gorda Cay Development. We discussed our options and concluded it was safer to go ashore than to try to leave. We jumped into the dinghy and motored ashore.

After entering the shack, we got the story from Bruce and Jeff. They asked us if we had seen the sunken boat, and explained that it was a single handler who had run up on the shore only a week ago. They were told that the insurance company insisted that it be left as it was for them to complete their investigation. They also told us of another incident where people from Andros had their motor launch burned at anchor. We didn't question that. At that time, Andros was also a hot bed of drug activity. There were usually three people on the island for two weeks, but one of them was flown out for his birthday. They also explained that a plane came in with supplies on a regular basis and to bring in their relief.

The architectural drawings were on the wall, and I could see that they had been there for some time because they had yellowed and had fly dirt all over them. Bruce took Pat and me out to see the airstrip while Jeff entertained the kids. They fed us a tasty dinner of barbecued chicken with rice and asparagus, and we watched a movie on a VHS video player, which was a new experience for us. The movie was *The Deep*, which involved a drug dealer. Needless to say, we were a little uncomfortable.

We all sauntered out to the dinghy for our departure, and they asked us to come in the morning before leaving to say goodbye. Back on the boat, we had a post mortem about our evening and our hosts. Jeff had told the girls that he raced cars, which Julie responded to as she had been to most of my races and was well acquainted with the racing scene. She had asked him where he raced and did he race SCCA. She was convinced by the answers that he didn't race. We suspected they were in the middle of a drug operation.

The next morning, I decided to go alone to say goodbye. In the meantime, a fishing skiff from Sandy Point came over to us with three locals. They were very friendly and seemed like nice guys. I followed them into shore, but by the time I arrived, there appeared to be a confrontation, so I immediately returned to *Melissa II*, weighed anchor, hoisted sails, and took off for Moore's Island, which was less than a day's sail away.

If you Google Gorda Cay, you will learn what we suspected. In fact, when we completed our journey two years later and arrived in Victoria, British Columbia, I had done a number of interviews on radio and television. One was in Vancouver with a delightful young gal from a radio station who suggested we go down to English Bay, sit on a log on the beach, and conduct the interview. After a couple of hours of questions, she turned the recorder off and said, "Now, there has to be something you daren't tell me while recording. The microphone is turned off so this is just between you and me." I told her of our Gorda Cay experience.

A few weeks later, she called me and suggested I watch the six o'clock evening news. It reported that a plane had crashed in Tennessee. The pilot had parachuted out, but his chute didn't open and he was killed. An investigation revealed that drugs were often dropped; in fact, they discovered that drugs had been dropped from that plane just before the pilot jumped. They disclosed that the plane had come from Gorda Cay. I feel comfortable with this discussion now, because in 1983, the whole operation was closed down and arrests were made. Gorda Cay was purchased by the Walt Disney Company and renamed Castaway Cay, which serves as an exclusive port for the Disney Cruise Lines. The movie Splash with Tom Hanks was filmed there in 1984.

We heard another unsavoury story of a Chicago lawyer, on a fishing expedition with his son in the Exumas, who spotted a sailboat on the rocks. The skipper launched a dinghy for him and his son to investigate. They found what appeared to be a body in a garbage bag. They hurried back to the fishing boat and called the Coast Guard. They were instructed to stand by. The Bahamian Coast Guard arrived and found the body missing. They determined that the boat belonged to a man and wife recently retired and living on their boat. As I recall, the man was a well-known TV broadcaster living in Florida. They had a couple of friends with them at the time. None of the bodies were recovered. The boat was taken to storage for some time before it was turned over to the family, who had to pay storage fees. The Chicago lawyer was outraged about the incident and published articles in the newspaper at his own expense, discouraging people from going to The Bahamas.

We were catching lots of fish, but they were large barracuda so we threw them back because of the possibility of ciguatera poisoning. While the kids were doing school work, Pat and I dove with hopes of spearing dinner. We saw many lobsters, but the lobster season was closed. Fortunately we were able to spear a grouper for dinner.

Carrying on from Moore's Island, we anchored off Norman's Castle in Green Turtle Cay, mid – to north-end of Abaco. The Bahamas are perfect for gunkholing, like the Virgin Islands but more spread out. The fishing was different, in that you could spear and eat the fish. Had lobster season been open, we could have been living on lobster. I think of it as snorkeling for food, whereas in the Virgin Islands you are viewing colourful tropical fish.

We needed a layover of three days to get over the Gorda Cay fright and generally get the ship in order to sail on to Beaufort, NC. Also, I had to get back to studying my ham radio in order to get my license, which was essential for us to have for communication while crossing the Atlantic Ocean. We chose Basin Harbour Cay with its picturesque jagged rocky cliffs along the west shore. It was the perfect spot. We were completely by ourselves. While the girls continued to do their school work, we hung out on the beach or did some chores. I did some repairs on Ned, our wind-activated self-steering device that we had to get in perfect order for our offshore adventure.

It was our intention to head north between Grand Bahama and Abaco, but on studying the chart, I saw that there wasn't enough depth. Consequently, we had to head back to Moore's Island then go south of Grand Bahama. We fetched an anchorage early evening, and the next morning celebrated Easter with bacon and eggs for breakfast. It was flat calm with not a ripple in the water, and we went for a dinghy ride like none other we had experienced before. The water was only about six feet deep and so crystal clear that it was like flying low over a field in an airplane. Five miles out there was a sandy beach on a small island, and a tiny, dry lagoon where we recovered a bucket of sea salt. There was also a fifty-foot-diameter tidal pool that a shark had swum into and couldn't get out. It was swimming around in circles. I had no doubt that it would be able to escape when the wind created a bit of a swell.

We weighed anchor at 0800 hours, with light winds from the south-west. It was goodbye to the Bahamas and hello to twenty-four-hour watches again. Our course was just a little north of west, so we hanked on a 150% genoa and reefed the main. By 1900 hours, we were abeam of Freeport. Once we cleared the west tip of Grand Bahama Island, we would be heading north in the favourable direction of the Gulf Stream.

For the next two days, we experienced light variable wind and had to rely on the motor for a few hours during the day. My sextant sites put us in the middle of the Gulf Stream and about 120 miles offshore. Abeam of Cape Canaveral, we started to see an electrical storm passing in front of us. During Pat's watch at around 0500 hours, things took a turn for the worse: winds increased to 40 knots from the north, and the seas grew to enormous heights. When winds are strong against the Gulf Stream, seas are steep and almost square. It brought Pat to tears because it was almost a repeat of the storm we had experienced last fall south of Bermuda. We had to turn and run with the wind for the next few hours, erasing all the progress we had made during the night. It was very discouraging, but as it turned out, short-lived.

As the day progressed, the wind veered to a favourable direction, and we poled out the genoa on one side with the main on the other, sailing wing on wing. It was amazing how quickly things turned around. We saw large grey porpoises in our bow wave leading us. We recalled having seen them the previous year, and after consulting my log, I discovered that it was the same area where we had encountered them before.

About one hundred miles from Charleston, SC, we decided to put in to take on diesel fuel after motoring a lot. Conditions were good, with favourable light winds throughout the day, which was a relief after the storm. By midnight, when we were less than a quarter of a mile from the harbour entrance, I tried to start the motor. It was sucking air, as the number three tank was dry. I still had a full tank to switch to but had to bleed the fuel injectors, which wasn't easy in rough seas. Pat had to sail back and forth avoiding ship traffic, while I struggled to bleed the air out of the system, her constantly screaming for me to hurry things along making matters all the more difficult. It was dark, and we couldn't see any room at the fuel dock, so we anchored for the rest of the night.

Early the next morning, we fueled up, found a spot at the marina, cleared customs and immigration, and had a restful few days enjoying Charleston. Founded in 1670, it was first named Charles Towne after the King of England. Julie was studying American history for her school assignment and was thrilled to be where the first shot had started the Civil War. I suggested she join me in the cockpit and pointing I said, "That is Fort Sumter!" It was all such a timely coincidence.

We toured the city by bus, visiting the museum and many gracious old colonial homes. People were very friendly and initiated conversations, asking us where we were from and what brought us to Charleston. When leaving a coin laundry, a black man ran up behind me saying, "You dropped your wallet," and handed it to me. It is not surprising that Charleston received "Top Destination in the World" by *Condé Nast Travelers* 2012 Readers' Choice Awards.

Back at the dock, everyone was discussing the recent storm. Jim Griffith, captain on *Delfino II,* a motor launch over 200 feet long, was delivering the boat from England for a syndicate and had been a professional captain most of his life. He said he was in the Gulf Stream as we were and the seas were tossing him to the extent that he feared losing the ship. In all his sailing, he had not seen it that severe. When the wind is from the north against the south-flowing current, you get the steep square-sided waves. It just strengthened my opinion that a thirty-foot boat was best for those conditions because it tosses around on top of the waves like a cork instead of burying itself into them. We spent the evening gamming with Ira and Kate aboard *White Hawk*, a Cherubini 44; Dick Cross aboard *Concord*, a Rhodes 50; and Scott aboard *Immigrant*.

Just after noon the next day, we cleared the jetty behind *White Hawk* and *Concord*: all heading for Beaufort. As the day progressed, we picked up on *White Hawk*, but as the wind dropped, she started motoring and pulled ahead. Julie and I were on the midnight to 0400 watch, and there was lots of activity to keep us awake. When three boats depart at the same time for the same destination, it's a race. We had lots of sail changes to keep us going at maximum speed.

We radioed *White Hawk* later in the day and discovered that she was behind us. We also talked to *Concord*, and she was well offshore and behind as well. We entered the harbour and dropped anchor at 0400 hours. *Concord* then came in, followed by *Night Hawk* about 0900 hours. It was not a great passage but fun to rendezvous with our new sailor friends in Charleston and visit Charles and his staff at the Beaufort Mariner's Museum.

All my energy was devoted to preparing for the ham radio exam. I took the bus to Norfolk Virginia to write the exam. *I flunked*, and I had to wait a month before I could write it again. I was so disappointed and furthermore it meant that we wouldn't be able to leave for our cross-Atlantic trip until late June. The incidence of storms in the North Atlantic increases to, on average, one every ten days in July, and I had to pass my exam to maintain contact with the outside world. I studied as I had in university days. Morse code was most of the problem. I studied from tapes and was humiliated by Jennifer, who was catching on faster than I was. I recall her correcting me on occasion: "R, Daddy, dit dot dit. That's R." I'm sure she would have passed the Morse code part of the exam. I understand that it is no longer required for a ham radio license.

We hung out in Beaufort for another month before I could write the exam again. In the meantime, I purchased a Drake TR-7, a solid-state amateur band transceiver enabling us to receive weather broadcasts and transmit. Then it was off to Norfolk by bus to write my exam again. *This time I passed!* Now I was KA4

2GM. My friends remembered it as KA4 Too Good to Miss. I was referred to Bill, a fellow ham in Florida who had heard about our trip and proposed that we schedule a daily contact during the voyage through the Maritime Network. We agreed on 2300 hours Greenwich Mean Time (GMT), or 1800 hours his time. As for us, it varied throughout our trip. It was really reassuring to know that we were going to be monitored during our crossing.

CHAPTER 8
Crossing the Atlantic

"He that will not sail till all dangers are over must never put to sea."

– Thomas Fuller

It has long been a superstition that it is bad luck to "put to sea on a Friday." Our friends gathered together at Omar Sails for a bon voyage pizza dinner on Friday. Back to the boat just before midnight, we immediately prepared for departure, complying with the superstition. Even though we had a month to prepare, there were still many last-minute things to accomplish before we weighed anchor at 0200 hours Saturday, June 20, 1981, heading for Cork, Ireland, via Bermuda and the Azores. We were guessing it would take a month.

We plunged into a rampant Gulf Stream with force 6 winds and blinding rain squalls that persisted for the next three days. Crashing seas filled our cockpit. With no moon, it was pitch black. We were all a bit apprehensive; the first night we started with Pat and Jennifer on the first watch, but Julie and I stayed in the cockpit. Julie got sick, which was very unusual for her. It was probably nerves. We were crossing the Gulf Stream and were being set north of our rhumb line, so I was guessing at the amount that we were being pushed off course. I began taking sextant shots, which was normal procedure, starting at 0900 hours then continuing all day until 1600 hours. We carried two inexpensive plastic sextants (metal ones are subject to corrosion). After dark, I would take moon and star shots. Calculating our position consumed a lot of time using the sight reduction tables, but I was a fanatic about knowing our exact position at all times.

As the first few days passed, we began to feel we were at sea again. We always had a fishing line dragging along behind us. At one point, we caught something so large it took our lure, hook, line, and bungee cord. After resetting our line, we caught a dorado that served us for a few meals. We were estimating that it would take five days to reach Bermuda. The only calamity we experienced was on the third day out when Ned (our wind-activated self-steering system) broke. Fortunately I had rigged up an Autohelm 1000, a 12-volt self-steering device designed for a tiller, to operate on my wheel with a tractor steering knob. It worked perfectly and had the added benefit that it could work while motoring. It took us across the Atlantic without us ever having to man the helm. The advantage of electric self-steering is that it operates under power as well as under sail. The disadvantage is that sail trim suffers a bit as you are inclined to over-trim to prevent the chance of luffing with the wave action.

We entered the harbour at St. George in Bermuda at 0200 hours, exactly five days to the hour from our start, having covered the 665 miles at a creditable rate of 133 miles a day. The discomforts of crossing the Gulf Stream were forgotten once these statistics were compiled. Even at that early hour, there was mass confusion in the harbour because the Marion to Bermuda Race participants were just crossing the finishing line. It is an event held every two years. The yachts were arriving from Marion, Massachusetts, and were filling the harbour. We anchored and hoisted our yellow flag (quarantine flag) to notify authorities that we required clearance. They immediately came out, even though it was the middle of the night.

Beautiful Bermuda is an offshore British Colony, although it was discovered in 1505 by a Spaniard, who it was named after. Among other things, it is famous for Bermuda shorts, which have been acceptable business wear since the early 1940s. This resulted from shortages of material for clothing during the war and suited the island climate. What I really enjoyed about Bermuda was that most cars were old British models in remarkable condition, with extremely low mileage, because there is only twenty miles of road end to end. Of the 200 islands, only twenty are inhabited. When we were there in 1980, you could be ticketed if your car was dirty and body repairs hadn't been done within a few days of an accident.

We found the locals very friendly, and we socialized with boaters who were also en route. *Westwind* was a barque we had seen in Tortola, BVI. *Rainbow*, a Cascade 29, was planning to leave in a day or two, and *Vangard*, a Pearson 32, expected to leave a week after us. *Namaste*, a forty-eight-foot trawler that had attempted the trip to Europe, ran into bad weather a couple of days out of Bermuda and decided to abandon the idea and return to the Bahamas. One of their crew members was a real character. When they docked, he jokingly asked a passerby: "What island is this?" *Jester,* a twenty-six-foot junk-rigged sailboat, formerly belonged to the famous single-handed sailing racer, Blondie Hasler, who is also credited with devising the first wind-activated self-steering system. The one I built was based on his design. He subsequently sold his boat to Mike Richey, with whom we discussed the best route to England. He decided to take the Great Circle route to Falmouth, England, and departed two days before us, with five weeks' wine supply. We didn't see him in England but are quite certain of two things: he made it, and he didn't follow the Great Circle route. The prevailing winds would not have allowed it. We became quite familiar with the North Atlantic weather patterns, and I'm afraid poor old Mike had more than his share of headwinds. We got them too! Years later, we heard that *Jester* had been lost in a storm in the North Atlantic. There was no mention of anyone being lost, so hopefully Mike was okay.

After a three-day stay, we departed late morning for the Azores, some 1,834 miles away, not knowing what to expect with the weather except that we would be sailing through a high pressure ridge stretching from Bermuda to the Azores. As it turned out, winds varied in direction, so we were unable to steer the rhumb line for days. We were tacking every few hours through huge seas. It was very stuffy in the cabin because we kept the hatches closed to avoid splashing seas. Needless to say, we suffered from seasickness. Sextant shots could only be done with me standing high on the life raft and holding onto the mast to sight the horizon. A fairlead snapped with a loud bang, necessitating me to jimmy rig repairs in dreadful conditions. The stitching was disintegrating around the batons on the main and had to be sewed. Everything takes so much longer at sea.

After a week, things gradually improved, although we had been pushed eighty miles off course. Our spirits improved; wind direction allowed us to reach on a starboard tack for a few days and, from time to time, veered behind us. It allowed us to set the spinnaker, increasing our speed to make up lost time. We heard radio reports that a tropical storm over Virginia was moving out over the North Atlantic. I was terrified! It brought to mind a Samuel Johnson's quote: "Sailing is long periods of boredom interspersed with periods of absolute fear."

There was more bad news. Our friends Hank and Sam, returning to Beaufort from Bermuda, were reported thirteen days overdue and a search had been called, while 150 miles north of us it was reported that a small tanker was sinking.

Sight taking with Sextant

Two large yellowfin tunas, in the 500-pound range, swam alongside, circling us from time to time. They would appear now and again throughout each day for a week, so close I felt I could have reached down and touched them. I guess they were just curious. When we were in Souris, Prince Edward Island, it was during the tuna season. When tuna were caught, they were cleaned, put in a casket, and shipped airfreight to Japan, fetching a price in the thousands of dollars.

We didn't encounter much ship traffic, but once when Julie was in the galley making sandwiches for lunch, she was startled to see a ship alongside at less than fifty feet away from us. I turned on the VHF radio and was greeted by the captain. He offered us a forty-five-gallon drum of diesel fuel and food supplies. We didn't need either, but we had a long conversation, as he was curious about our passage. He was on his way to New York City. I pointed out that he was aimed in the wrong direction. He said that he had picked us up on his radar and so came off course to investigate. Along with his passengers and crew, they lined up on the starboard side waving, yelling greetings, and taking pictures.

Wind direction varied over the next few days but was generally light, allowing us to drag out all the upholstery and bedding to dry. We got the news that Hank and Sam were rescued and were under tow to Beaufort by the Coast Guard.

Sam had suffered two broken ribs, yet, it was just such a relief to hear that they were safe. Then news arrived that the tanker that had been in distress had sank, however, all aboard were rescued safely.

Our lives were getting back to normal. There were always lots of chores, including sail repairs, checking the rigging, and tuning the engine, which I would often run to charge our batteries. When transmitting on the radio, a lot of power is required. Julie and Jennifer took part in the navigation, wrote letters to their friends, did their watches with us, and helped with the sail repairs. Julie was the galley maid, and Jennifer was charged with polishing the brass.

The next period of excitement came when we spotted eight sperm whales all sailing single file in the opposite direction to us. The last one I was guessing to be a male. He was about sixty feet long, with eyes about a foot in diameter. He looked over at us and gradually altered course ninety degrees to steer directly for us. I was terrified, while Pat and the girls were in the cockpit, thrilled with the experience. Within a boat length of us, it altered course to join its pod. Sperms are the largest toothed whales. Its big head, which makes up a third of its length, is full of spermaceti oil that made them valuable to whalers. It gives them the ability to dive down almost two miles, where they feed on giant squid. They can be aggressive. *Moby Dick*, by Herman Melville, is based on the true story of a Nantucket whaling vessel being attacked by a sperm whale while whaling in the Pacific. With whales being virtually extinct in the Nantucket area by the mid-1800s, whalers were forced to round Cape Horn to get to the Pacific to continue whaling.

Since this was before the Panama Canal was built, the only route was around the Horn. Whales sleep with one eye open and just their noses out of the water. My fear of running into one was intensified by the fact that we were in an area where sperm whales were prevalent. In 1980, whaling was still carried out in the Azores. The thought of a wounded one attacking us was always on my mind.

We were now within 300 miles from the Azores. I tried contacting the UK's Maritime Network. They could hear me but couldn't make out my call letters. Pat heard that they were predicting strong winds from the east, the exact direction we were headed. When winds increased to force 6 with twenty-foot waves, we were only able to split 120 degrees on our tacks, instead of normal ninety degrees or less. We were now looking at five days to get to the Azores instead of the three that we had hoped for. We were down to storm jib and trysail and were all very discouraged. The cabin and everything in it was drenched. Our position indicated that we had only advanced thirty miles in one day.

As the day progressed, the wind went down and our spirits went up. Even the wind direction became more favourable from the south, so we were on a reach with full main and 140% genoa. I was asleep, so Pat was faced with sail changes and bagging them. Then we started getting into traffic. The skipper on the Danish vessel *Falstria*, headed for Vancouver, altered course to say hello and chat. He gave us his position, which was spot-on with ours. Next contact was with *Jay Gour* of Bombay, who altered their course for Philadelphia to have a look at us and inquire about our daily routine and ultimate destination. We were obviously in the shipping lanes because next was *Rio Chone* from Ecuador taking a load of bananas to Cork, Ireland. We didn't get close enough to see him, but the skipper seemed excited about our adventure and asked lots of questions. We promised to visit him in Cork. It was a thrill to talk to these people, and we hoped to connect with them for a face-to-face visit in port.

The archipelago of the Azores, an autonomous region of Portugal, comprises nine volcanic islands stretching 370 miles. Horta on Faial is the major port. In 1957, the volcano Capelinhos erupted, forming a new island that joins Faial. Consequently, if you were using a pre-1957 chart, you would be quite confused when approaching from the west, as the new island would not be shown. The islands were first settled by Flemish and Portuguese in 1439. Although we didn't speak any Portuguese, the inhabitants were very charming and anxious to help.

We moored at Ponta Delgada which had many old stone buildings, cobblestone streets, and sidewalks inlaid with patterns of black volcanic rock. The stonework was incredible. In fact, many bricklayers in Canada and the US are Portuguese from the Azores. The streets were so neat and tidy. In the country, there were no fences. Farm animals were tethered, and we were welcome to walk through farmers' fields. As whaling was still practiced, it was not surprising that we came across one corral that used sperm whale lower jaw bones for fence posts. Trees were virtually non-existent. Every square inch of land – including roadside ditches – was planted with fruits and vegetables. Crops are often fertilized with night soil (human waste), which can be associated with parasitic worms (helminthes) in humans. Pharmaceutical companies will often conduct studies for their antihelminthics in the Azores where parasitic worms are quite prevalent. The beaches of black volcanic sand are virtually impossible to walk on in bare feet because of the heat from the sun.

We departed at 1700 hours, the same time as Will and Jenny aboard *Gimble* left for Portugal. If you are heading for the UK, it's a good idea to get north as quickly as possible to eventually catch the westerlies. The ocean between the Azores and the English Channel experiences nine times more gales than the rest of the North Atlantic. This, coupled with my notion that north is always uphill, did little to my eagerness to start the final leg of our crossing. In spite of easterly winds, we were able to sail our rhumb line of fifty-seven degrees. Within two hours, winds increased to force 7 from the north-east. How quickly conditions can change! Because skies were overcast for the next three days, we were compelled to use our DR. We got our position from *Spray,* a small freighter bound for Greenland with a load of salt. It was eighty miles from what I had tracked with our DR. I was a little suspicious of it and didn't alter course. When I finally was able to get some sun shots, it confirmed our DR was on track.

Our next encounter with a ship occurred the following day with *Indian Ocean,* a fine-looking vessel 148 metres in length had a speed of 22 knots. The captain, who spoke broken English, was very friendly and told us he was loaded with cargo from Germany and heading for Miami. He also confirmed that our DR position was correct. For the next six days the winds howled between force 4 and 10. There was no moon! When it was pitch black, I often got disoriented and leapt over to the compass, thinking we were headed in the wrong direction. One night, I was convinced we were sinking and shone the light down below expecting to see the cabin sole under water. It wasn't. The light alerted Julie, and she bounded out the companion saying, "What's going on!" She sensed that I was a little confused. The seas now appeared green rather than blue, and at night we were getting lots of phosphorescence in our wake, something we hadn't seen since leaving the North Pacific.

As daylight approached, we saw a new type of porpoise: grey with a white underside. We also sighted a picnic table floating just below the surface. It was providing a home for groupers, plus many other species of various sizes. The weather turned cold. Radio propagation was poor, so we weren't able to QSO with Bill or the British Maritime Marine network for the next two days. As it turned out, the antenna connection was corroded. After I stripped the wire and soldered a new connection, we finally got through. The radio operator from the Maritime Marine was surprised when I told him our vessel was *Melissa ll.* He replied that the Coast Guard had been notified that we were sick and hadn't been heard from for a few days. It is true that, during a QSO (amateur radio contact) with Bill, I told him we were all sick, and I suspected that we had probably picked up something from the water in the Azores and we had switched to our emergency water supply. Apparently another amateur radio operator in Bermuda, following our progress, notified the Coast Guard, which began a North Atlantic-wide search, alerting all vessels. Needless to say, I was a little embarrassed.

Next we ran into a real 'gear buster', horrendous winds gusting to force 8 from the north. We were not making any headway under trysail and storm jib and were forced to abandon our plan of reaching Cork. We were only sixty miles away and could actually see Fastnet Rock, but the strong winds were against us. The 1979 Fastnet Yacht Race experienced horrendous winds; twenty-five boats were lost, resulting in eighteen fatalities. This was heavily on our minds while we were experiencing similar conditions, so we altered course for Falmouth, England. It was very discouraging, more so for Pat who had spent the entire day before sewing an Irish courtesy flag in less than ideal conditions.

Land's End finally came into view at 0710 hours. We turned on our VHF radio and almost immediately heard them calling the *Melissa ll.* They inquired about the state of our health and wanted to know our ETA for landfall. We told them Falmouth and estimated it would be 1500 hours. They said to call when we were at the harbour entrance and that immigration, customs, and health authorities would be there to welcome us. We were in the English Channel and only hours away from completing our crossing of the Atlantic.

We anchored at 1600 hours, August 2, 1981, hoisted our British courtesy flag along with our yellow quarantine flag, and in minutes were greeted by all the Falmouth authorities. They required a sample of our water and requested urine and stool samples from all of us before they could grant permission to go ashore. After only a matter of hours, they confirmed that we were okay. We got ashore, and I immediately kissed the ground. There was no question that this leg was the worst. It took twelve days, twenty-three hours to cover the 1,412 miles from the Azores, which works out to a meager 109 miles a day, but we had crossed the Atlantic! In retrospect, it was a relatively successful and quick passage. It took us thirty-four days, nine and a half hours to cover the 3,911 miles from Beaufort to Falmouth, England. The weather was cold; we struggled to keep on moving east; we were all sick, and we were forced to alter course to go to Falmouth, not our original destination of Cork, Ireland.

CHAPTER 9
Jolly Old England

"Now, if you huff and puff you finally save enough money up to take your family on a trip across the sea, Take a tip before you take a trip, let me tell you where to go, Go to England, Oh."

– Song by Roger Miller

Falmouth, the most southwesterly harbour in Great Britain, was often the port for the start and finish for world-renowned sailors like Sir Francis Chichester and Sir Robin Knox Johnston, who both sailed solo around the world. It is the home of the Royal Cornish Yacht Club formed in 1871. News of Nelson's death and his great victory at the Battle of Trafalgar in 1805, where he defeated Napoleon, first arrived in Falmouth aboard the vessel HMS *Pickle*. In 1836, Charles Darwin aboard HMS *Beagle* anchored in the harbour following his survey voyage around the world.

Falmouth Harbour, Welcome to jolly ol' England

We spent the week walking the streets of Falmouth and enjoying the company of fellow yachtsmen. Tides range up to eighteen feet in the harbour, making dinghy landing quite difficult. It did not deter us from daily visits, shopping, enjoying fish and chips and just walking the streets. It was amusing to see a teahouse that had a sandwich board with a chalked sign announcing, "Lovely lunch now being served." It is an expression Pat and the kids have had to endure me repeating often to this day. There was a contingent of Cornish Crabbers, a traditional sailing craft that happened to stage a race during our stay. Boats with twin keels, or bilge keels as they are called, are popular along the south coast because they can sit comfortably aground upright when the tide goes out.

Next was Plymouth, only thirty miles away. There was no wind so we motored. It was good battery charging weather. From the harbour, we had a view of the Royal Citadel, a majestic 17th century fortress built to protect the British coast from the Dutch invaders. We carried on to Brixham but only to anchor for the night before heading to Exmouth, where we left our boat for two weeks while touring southern England. We had chosen Exmouth because our friend Ken, back in Canada, insisted we contact his sister and her husband, Eleanor and Len Smith. They were wonderful hosts and were avid sailors to boot, belonging to the Exmouth Sailing Club.

One of the things on my to-do list of preparations for the canals in France was to somehow acquire several used tires to serve as fenders to protect *Melissa II's* topsides from the cement walls. It was our good fortune that Len had a tire shop! He supplied me with sixteen used tires. Interesting enough, a few yacht club members we met knew nothing about using the French canals to get to the Mediterranean. That surprised me, as they were just across the English Channel. They claimed the French canals were too shallow for a sailboat that drew six feet. English canals are only three feet deep, but we were well aware that the French ones were at least six feet deep to accommodate the *péniches*, the river/canal barges that transversed the canals, transporting goods and services like our eighteen-wheelers do in North America.

After renting a Ford Fiesta for two weeks, we started off on our land venture. We visited Castle Combe, a small village in Wiltshire, home of a car racetrack converted from a World War II air force airport. It was where Stirling Moss began racing in a 500 cc formula car. Because it had been an airport, the track was very flat, of course, and very fast. No races were on during our visit, but we walked the track. In the town itself, no vehicle traffic was allowed. We heard the story that Thomas Blanket had lived there in a house by the stream and weaved wool into a cover to keep off the chill, thereby introducing the 'blanket'. I've heard other renditions, but I like that one the best. In 1966, Castle Combe was used in the filming of *Doctor Doolittle*.

Our friends in Toronto referred us to their relatives in Chippenham, John and Audrey Hickman, who were kind enough to take us on a tour of their 16th century home. I couldn't help but notice an engine block upside down on the basement floor and said, "What are you doing with a Fiat engine?" He was shocked that I knew what it was, and it launched us into petrol-head talk. He was very envious that we were headed to the Morgan Motor Company plant in Malvern Link the next morning, even though it was only fifty miles away and he would have been able to go anytime, but he was reluctant to do so as he didn't want to appear nosy. He was a jeweler who made jewelry for the Queen of England, yet he felt it would have been imposing for him to visit the Morgan Factory. Peter Morgan, the founder's son, was very hospitable and knew of my racing endeavours in Canada. He insisted I drive his turbo-charged Plus 8 in the morning, and then his wife, Heather, insisted I drive her Morgan 4/4 after lunch. Both Peter and his son Charles were enthusiastic sailors and flooded us with questions about our Atlantic crossing. We had lunch at the Morgan Pub in town before returning to the plant for the afternoon.

We visited Stonehenge and the Baths before eventually making our way to London. Apart from the usual tourist attractions, we went to Greenwich Royal Observatory, which established Greenwich Mean Time, an average of the time the sun is at its highest point over Greenwich. It also establishes zero degrees longitude. It is a real challenge to calculate your longitude at sea, and using a sextant is not as accurate as calculating latitude, which is observed from the greatest angle of the sun at noon.

We attended a sports car race at Brands Hatch. I had heard about this track and was thrilled to see a Morgan win the event because I had raced a Morgan for many years in Canada. The track was hilly and had the characteristics of Mosport Park, the Ontario racetrack where I did most of my competing.

Eventually we returned to the boat; it was like being back at home. Out came the charts, and we drew up our plan to proceed along the coast to Portsmouth, with stops along the way. We docked at Poole to phone my mother. During

World War II, Poole was an important departing point for the D-Day landings in the Normandy invasion.

While having our lunch on board, a young boy pointed out to his father, "Look! There's a boat from Canada!" "They would have had it shipped here," said his father. I wanted to call out that "we had sailed here", however, I refrained from doing so.

A few days later we reached Portsmouth and were surprised to see so many boats at anchor outside the harbour. We discovered they were spectator boats waiting to see the start of the Whitbread Round the World Race, which takes place every three years. Whitbread was a brewing company. In 2001, Volvo took over the race and renamed it the Volvo Round the World Race. It was quite a coincidence and our good fortune that we arrived just in time for the start. One spectator's boat we recognized from seeing it in the Virgin Islands and in the Azores. There was a lot of excitement as the flag dropped and the gun went off. Many spectator yachts had to abandon their anchors to get out of the way of the competitors. They marked the anchor lines with floats so they could retrieve them after the competitors had passed. By early afternoon, it was all over, and we fetched a mooring to enjoy a day of sightseeing, touring the HMS *Victory*, Horatio Nelson's ship that has been in dry dock as a tourist attraction since 1922.

CHAPTER 10
The Canals of France

"If one does not know to which port one is sailing, no wind is favourable."

– Seneca

We left the Camper Nicholson fuel dock in Portsmouth at 1645 hours in brisk winds to cross the English Channel to the French coast. The wind piped up to force 6, making the voyage faster than we had anticipated. We hove to at the Le Havre Light Vessel as it was still dark and too early to make an entrance to Honfleur or Le Havre. We chose Le Havre and followed dozens of cardinal beacons that mark navigable waters by compass bearings. After clearing customs and immigration, we began our preparation for the canals. Fortunately, there was a hoist for dropping the mast, which we did, setting it on a cradle that I made up of 2x4s picked up at the lumberyard. We put our used tires in blue garbage bags and strung them from the gunnels as fenders to protect our topsides from the concrete canal walls.

Le Havre is often referred to as the *city without a soul*. During the Battle of Normandy in World War II, the British obliterated it when it was occupied by the Germans. Ninety percent of the city was reduced to rubble. Today, it represents a city that was built in the 50s and 60s using the latest materials and design. Although beautiful, it lacks the old churches and buildings that give a French city character. It is located at the mouth of the Seine River, which is navigable by large ships as far as Rouen. Our trip was going to be from the English Channel to the Mediterranean through the entire length of France from north to south. We weren't even guessing how long it was going to take. All we knew was that we were leaving early that day, September 4, 1981.

Ready for the French Canals

It was 0845 hours when we rushed to the mouth of the Seine to take advantage of the flooding tide. We fought our way up the river against the tide until noon when it started flooding, giving us a boast. I was expecting the river to be heavily industrialized. It wasn't! In fact, the trip was breathtaking, meandering along with high wooded cliffs, quaint little French villages and acres of farmland on both sides of the river. We passed an abbey dating back to the 7th century and encountered ship and péniche traffic until reaching Rouen at 1930 hours. Initially we tied up to a city wall. A local sailor, advised us to move to a protected basin around the corner that would be much quieter.

We spent a couple of days in Rouen, absorbing the beautiful buildings including the cathedral, which replaced a church that was built in the 4th century. Despite its history of bombardment and reconstruction, it was the most beautiful building I had ever seen and was visible from anywhere in the city. The Place du Vieux Marché is where Joan of Arc was burned at the stake in 1431 when she was 19 years old. She led a small French army to many victories against the English during the Hundred Years' war. At her execution, British officers had tears in their eyes because they had such a high regard for her military achievements. We walked up La Route de la Corniche where the views of the city were fabulous, a great place to take photos.

The traffic in the Seine started at 0500 hours even though it was still dark. Initially we noticed a lot of pollution both in the air and in the water. We passed the city of Elbeuf, a heavily industrialized area with lots of factories and from the canal we could see the Renault car factory. Once we encountered our first lock, the river was more tranquil and had lots of lovely homes on both sides.

We anchored across from the town of Les Andelys, home of Château Gaillard, built in 1196 on a cliff overlooking the Seine by Richard the Lionheart, who was the Duke of Normandy as well as King of England. You could see why he chose this location. It is perched high on a rock looking down on the river and strategically placed to impede advancing forces. It was to prevent the French from reaching Rouen. Nonetheless, it failed to resist the attacks of the French King Philippe Auguste in 1204. During the Hundred Years War, it was retaken by the English, then the French, then the English, ad infinitum. I'm enthralled by the history of France. As a Canadian, I'm just not exposed to ancient history. We did a walkabout in the early evening. There was practically no traffic, and all the homes had their shutters closed, with few lights visible, just like in the blackouts during World War II. This was 1981, and I hope it hasn't changed much since. There were no neon signs, no McDonald's, and no KFC. I wish we had stayed longer, but we were quite excited about our venture through the waterways of France, and there was pressure to just keep going.

Vernon was only fifteen miles away and only one lock from Les Andelys, well known for its production of aircraft engines. We enjoyed a day of rest, anchored near a 12th century bridge with an old mill on the bank, and saw a 12th century church and a wood-frame house built next door. Claude Monet, a founder of French impressionism, lived in Giverny, walking distance from Vernon. His garden, a spectacular tourist attraction, inspired many of his paintings. Our next stop was Limay, where we tied up to a municipal pontoon, and were getting accustomed to, "Hey what's the rush? Let's just lay over for a few days." It is across the Seine from Mantes-la-Jolie where William the Conqueror, also known as the King of Normandy, defeated the French and set fire to the town then fell off his horse and died. Poetic justice, I guess.

We met an enthusiastic sailor who lived on a péniche that he had converted into his home. He took us on a tour, and it was gorgeous. The kitchen was beautifully done in mosaic tile. Below deck, in the main living area, high on the wall, the perimeter was graced with a Bayeux Tapestry replica depicting the history of France, which had been done by his mother. We saw our first criterium, a bike race of many laps held on a short course (usually less than one mile), run on closed-off city centre streets. Years later, I was co-chairman of the Bastion Square Cycling Festival in downtown Victoria, BC, which included a criterium. During my race, I relived the one I had seen in France.

We departed Limay in company with *Nordlys* and *Wild Sage,* a Nicholson 32 with Larry and wife, Barry, onboard. They had arrived at Limay the previous night and we quickly became good friends. In fact, we travelled most of the trip to the Mediterranean with them. After one lock, we tied up at a pontoon at Andrésy, which looked like it was a resting spot for empty péniches waiting to be loaded and dispatched. The basin was full of them. We arrived to a downpour of rain which put a damper (no pun intended) on our walking tour. It was also quite chilly. On overnight stops, we tied up to a pontoon if there was one, or just pulled up along the side of the canal and tied to a tree. I had built a ladder out of 2x4s to use as a ramp to get to shore if we couldn't get close enough. As was often the case, we started the day picking up baguettes or croissants for breakfast, then off we'd go. The next thirty miles were a mixed bag from luxurious homes to slum areas of trailer homes with garbage sliding down to the Seine. We saw a lot of houseboats and live-aboard ferrocement sailboats that didn't look like they had ever sailed. Eventually we found a pontoon to accommodate all three of us. Even though it was pouring rain, we walked down as far as the Arc de Triomphe de l'Étoile, which honours those who fought and died for France in the French Revolution and the Napoleonic Wars. Beneath its vault lies the Tomb of the Unknown Soldier from World War I.

I can't begin to describe the history of Paris. With my obsession of history, I was dumbfounded. On the way to our next anchorage, we passed the Statue of Liberty. It is a replica of the original in New York, a gift from France in 1886 that depicts United States' independence gained in 1776. The French didn't have a lot of regard for Britain in those days, and they applauded the fact that the Americans had won their independence.

With only eleven miles to go, we reached the Touring Club of France in downtown Paris by noon. We rafted to a péniche located by the Alexander III Bridge, which was quite a spot!

The bridge is a work of art graced with sculptures of four gilt-bronze statues at each corner. The Eiffel Tower loomed overhead. Moorage fees were only five dollars a day, including hot water showers, mail and friendly suggestions for must-see attractions. We were just down the bank from the Champs-Élysées with the Arc de Triomphe de l'Étoile at one end and Place de la Concorde at the other. The Musée du Louvre, the largest and most visited museum in the world, was only a short walk away and the number and the age of the displays astonished us. There were artifacts from the Nile civilizations dating from 4,000 BC to the 4th century; the Mona Lisa painted by Leonardo da Vinci in 1503; the sculpture of Venus de Milo, believed to have been done in 150 BC and thousands of other pieces of art. We spent the entire day realizing we could spend many more absorbing its splendour.

The perfect mooring for Paris

Also while in Paris, we celebrated Julie's fourteenth birthday, having promised her a birthday in Paris when we left to cross the Atlantic. We had planned to have Julie and Jennifer's year of school work sent to the Canadian Embassy in Paris. They were excited to get their new year of books and began studying the day we picked them up. It was fortunate they were so enthusiastic about their studies. As we discovered, that wasn't always the case with other boaters' children. During our summer in Ontario, we arranged to have Julie and Jennifer meet their teacher who had marked all their correspondence. It was very exciting for them, and they just loved her. She was more of a friend to them than a teacher.

We did a lot of our sightseeing with Sid and Jeanine aboard *Malibu*, a converted péniche. Although their home was in Carmel, California, they spent a lot of time in Paris aboard their barge that was permanently moored in Paris. Jeanine was from Paris and was a great help for directions to get around. Our trusty inflatable dinghy was a Hutchison, manufactured in Bois-Colombes just north of Paris. Through wear and tear, it had developed air leaks, so we hopped on a bus with it on my shoulder and headed for the factory. They were very obliging and assured me it would be ready in two days. Although we had no need for it in the canals, it was nice to know it would be like new when we hit the Mediterranean. Bois-Colombes is on the Seine, so we took the boat to pick it up, having made quite an effort lugging it on the bus. We rafted to a péniche for the night and the next morning, we returned to the Touring Club of France and rafted to *Wild Sage*. After lunch, we proceeded to the first lock after Paris, where there was a two-hour wait. We met friends from Portsmouth aboard *Procyon*, a Nicolson 35, bound for the Mediterranean. We both stopped alongside of the lock for the night. *Melissa II* was moving very slowly, and I couldn't figure out why. Since the transmission didn't seem to be slipping, I suspected it must have been growth on the propeller. At some point, I knew that I would have to jump in the dirty canal water and check it out.

We departed together the following morning for the next lock, which had sloped sides. Each with a line, Pat and Jennifer got off before we entered the lock, as it would have been impossible once inside it. They tied us to a bollard, then once the lock filled, it was simply a matter of stepping aboard. Our next stop was Melun. We walked the Île de la Cité, the island in the Seine in the centre of Paris, believed to have been settled in the 500s. It is the home of the Notre Dame de Paris, completed in the 1300s, that inspired Victor Hugo to write the novel *Hunchback of Notre Dame*.

Departing Melun the next morning, we ran aground. *Alnaga*, a péniche, pulled us off. It was a bit scary because rather than pull us off back in the direction we had come from, he pulled us forward over a much shallower area. We were very grateful to get underway again and sped up to the next lock to give the skipper a bottle of wine.

We had arranged to meet my sister Joan at Saint-Mammès. She was going to take the train from Paris, and I was to meet her at the station. I walked up to the station to find out the arrival time, which sounded like a fairly easy chore. *It wasn't!* In my best French, I explained to the station mistress that I was meeting my sister arriving from Paris and asked what time the train would arrive. It was very difficult for me to understand her, but she told me what she thought would be the arrival time.

Back at *Melissa II,* I resumed ship's chores and couldn't believe my luck when Keith from *Procyon* told me he was a diver and had a wetsuit that I was welcome to borrow to investigate the underside to see if I could determine the slow boat problem. Everything seemed fine, but I did give the propeller a scrub. It would be weeks later when I would learn that the knot meter was reading incorrectly and would require adjusting.

Later, I returned to the station at what I had understood to be the right time. Joan was there and had been waiting for me for two hours. Her French was fluent so she chatted with the station mistress who told her that this man had talked to her in the worst French she had ever heard, which I found odd because I understood every word I said! To Joan, that confirmed that I was in town. She was impressed with the condition of the boat; Jennifer had polished all the brass and Julie had cleaned and hung out all the upholstery to dry. One thing we had grown accustomed to with Joan's visits was her large wheeled suitcase, which was not suitable for storage on boats. We strapped it behind the mast on top of the life raft.

We were leaving the Seine and entering the Loire Canal system. It was similar to a fork in the road. This resulted in a huge amount of péniche traffic splitting off in both directions. After our usual breakfast of fresh croissants from the patisserie, we went for a pleasant walk, viewing the sights of Saint-Mammès before we left. At the first Canal du Loing, we chatted with the lock master, an engaging fellow who spoke perfect English and therefore escaped my French. He gave us books for navigating the canals that proved very useful. We were heading for Nemours, which we assumed would be our next overnight layover. After seven small manual and very picturesque locks that we operated ourselves, we arrived at the pretty little town. The girls were engulfed in their school work while we went for a walk. We passed the Château de Nemours built in 1120. It was the site of the signing of the Treaty of Nemours in 1585, which ratified the progress of the Catholic League and urged Protestants to leave the kingdom.

After fifteen self-managed locks, we arrived in Montargis, often referred to as Venice of the Gâtinais. In my mind, this was the prettiest town in France. The canal curves through town to the extent that you can't see an oncoming péniche. We were fortunate that a cyclist yelled, "Péniche là-bas," as we wouldn't have been able to see it.

Following a peniche through Montargis

When you encounter a péniche in the canal, you head for the wall or bank and hold on as the turbulence is extremely strong, even though they are only going three or four kilometers. There are numerous little canals not navigable by boat in Mortargis, branching off from the Seine but have small wooden dinghies decorated with flower arrangements. It is drenched in medieval history, probably most famous for the "Dog of Mortargis." The story goes that King Charles the V's courtier was murdered by a rascal who was decreed a trial by combat or duel with the courtier's dog. The dog won, and the rascal was hanged.

We tied up at a double lock for the night along with a couple from Edmonton, Alberta, who were on a tour barge. It was nice to abandon my dreadful French to speak English. We noticed an area of flat-deck barges that were for rent. You could park a travel trailer or caravan (as they are called in England) on it and, from a wheelhouse that looked like a phone booth, operate an outboard motor to transverse the canals. It looked like a great way to travel the canals, viewing them from a mobile trailer park.

We travelled through a heavily forested area on our way to Châtillon-Coligny, where we met two fellows from Bern, Switzerland, who were travelling in a rental barge for two weeks. For yachters on their own boats, passing through the locks was free of any charges, or it was then. If a lock keeper was present, we would often give him a bottle of wine. We passed a palatial old private home with a moat around it and a drawbridge to the front door.

Having done eight locks, we were ready for a stop and tied up just beyond a bridge. From the cockpit, I could see a men's public urinal that shielded users from the waist down. We were all quite fascinated with this, and I asked Pat to take a picture of me using it. Wouldn't you know! I couldn't go, but at least Pat got a good picture of me faking it. We often saw men urinating at bus stops throughout France. Even in Paris on the Champs-Élysées at rush hour, a gentleman dressed in a suit thought nothing of spinning around and urinating, so we wondered why they had bothered to build urinals. We passed the Napoleonic 16th century canal system that veers off to the east, very picturesque but not in use any more. We were held up for three and a half hours at the next lock because a movie was being filmed, so even after 18 locks, we didn't make it as far as Briare. We tied up against the wall for the night. It was a swampy area with nowhere to walk, which is what we enjoyed doing in the evenings.

Next morning – after only two locks that were taking us down – we reached Briare. Briare has a wonderful cathedral and a car museum that was closed unfortunately, a disappointment for me, as I'm sure there were some neat old models of Renaults, Citroens and Peugeots on display. Briare is also famous for the Water Bridge or viaduct over the Loire River. Designed by Gustave Eiffel in 1890 after he completed the Eiffel

Water Bridge over the Loire River

30 metres above the Loire River

Tower, it is about thirty metres above the river, and wide and deep enough for a péniche to cross. It is an unusual experience to be in a canal looking down at the river below. I stayed back and took pictures of Pat going over it. She was in constant fear that a péniche would appear and she would have to back up; not an easy task in a sailboat, but all was well.

Our next stop was Saint-Thibault, where we went on a long hike up to and climbed the Tour des Fiefs. Even in the rainy weather, it was a spectacular view over the Loire Valley with all the vineyards. Sancerre (the name was derived from "Sacred to Caesar") is surrounded by ramparts to protect the city. It was also the site of the infamous Siege of Sancerre (1572–1573) during the religious wars where the Huguenot population, who were Protestants, were confined by the city walls for nearly eight months by the Catholic forces of the king. They resorted to eating the leather soles of their shoes, rats, ground slate and some turned to cannibalism to stay alive. The Catholics were so impressed by the resistance offered by the Huguenots that they ameliorated them by letting them practice their religion.

Next, we visited the town of La Charité-sur-Loire on an island in the Loire River. After tying up along the canal wall, we walked more than a mile to cross over a bridge built in the 1500s to get to the town. During the religious wars, it suffered the same fate as Sancerre, in that the Huguenots withstood eight months of siege by Catholic forces while in Sainte-Croix-Notre-Dame, the second-largest cathedral in France that can shelter 5,000 people.

It was the first week of October, and we had no deadlines. We were so engrossed with the history and the quaintness of the little towns and villages that we hadn't even discussed how long it would take us to reach the Mediterranean. Some days we would transverse twenty locks, other days maybe two. It was incredible that a boater could travel across the entire country from north to south and transverse over 200 locks at no cost. The péniche captains were friendly and often invited us to raft alongside for the night. In many cases, it was their domicile with their wife and kids who, like ours, were home-schooled. They would have a small car on deck perpendicular to the length of the vessel, which they could launch to scoot around town.

On our way to Nevers, we stopped at Marseilles-lès-Aubigny, one of the few nondescript villages along the way. We couldn't get very close to the canal shore because it was too shallow, and we had to use our ladder as a ramp. We knew the next day was going to be a challenge because of the increase in péniche traffic. The canal was through a very picturesque wooded area. We went through two viaducts and had numerous close encounters with oncoming péniches and since it was their domain, it was up to us to keep out of their way.

We reached Nevers early afternoon where my sister would take the train to Paris to fly home. Naturally, it was sad to see her go, so before she left we managed to take her on a tour of the town. Each time we tied up, we would meet up with friends plus new people who were en route to the Mediterranean. It is hard to believe that Nevers dates back to 52 BC when Julius Caesar centred his Roman forces there before he was defeated by the Gauls. We walked the narrow streets lined with old homes dating back to the 14th century. It is incredible that they are still standing and serving as residences. The Notre Dame Cathedral had great examples of gargoyles, and I took many pictures. We visited a monument commemorating all the children who perished during the great wars and we stood on the bridge over the Loire River watching kayaks racing.

The next morning we made an early departure, encountering two locks that we shared with a young British couple who had spent eighteen months in Spain. The canal narrowed going through low-lying forests and pasture land. It was like driving a highway and looking down on farms along the way. The canals are a minimum of 2.2 metres deep to accommodate the draft of the péniches. In fact, the péniches help dredge the canal as they push the mud off to one side. For us, once you stray from the middle, you run aground. We had an unusual and scary incident when we encountered an oncoming péniche going full speed. We went off centre into the mud, but the péniche's wake sucked us over, listing us twenty degrees. Had he understood that I was hard aground off the centre line, he could have slowed.

We finally reached the lock at Decize where we saw the *Nordlys* crew filling up with water, so we did too. We had done eight locks; it was pouring rain so we called it a day, tied up to a tree, ramped ashore and walked into town. Decize is where Julius Caesar settled a dispute involving the Decetiae from whom the town gets its name. This occurred about 50 BC.

The wind screamed all night, blowing us hard aground. I had to winch us off in the morning before we got underway. It was windy, rainy and cold all day. We pushed through, covering forty miles by 1830 hours and doing sixteen locks. We stopped just past the viaduct or Water Bridge as they are called, at Digoin, not to be confused with Dijon, the land of the mustard. Pat and I did our evening walk in the pouring rain while the girls did their school work.

It was still raining the following morning so we endeavoured to get ahead of a péniche that we had gone through the last lock with; however, he was slower than usual. We were low on fuel and were getting air in the fuel line. I spent a lot of time buried in the engine compartment, bleeding out the air with Pat at the helm. Things did not improve during the day. We went under a bridge that was undergoing construction and had a string across the canal. It tore off our Canadian flag so we had to turn around in the narrow canal to retrieve it. Then we got into a jam with an oncoming fast-moving péniche. His wake sucked us towards him. I swung the wheel hard over to starboard and gave full throttle. Besides driving us another ten feet aground, our mast – which was horizontal over the cabin top extending aft – swept over his deck hitting his cabin top and knocking off some lines. I'm not sure who was angrier, but there certainly was nothing I could have done to avoid it.

The countryside was great, yet the stopovers weren't as interesting as those we had experienced earlier. In addition, the howling wind and driving rain wasn't helping matters, and while both of us stayed in the cockpit for steering and generally keeping an eye on things, it meant that we were exposed to the miserable conditions. Things improved as we encountered our first automatic locks and our first automatic lift bridge, and then searched for a place to spend the night. We had gone through twenty-one locks that day and finally settled down between two of them.

We were off at 0700 hours and encountered all electric locks. The lockmaster watched as we went through then drove his car to the next one. He did this for four locks before deciding we could handle them on our own. It was cold and windy, but at least it wasn't raining. The countryside was beautiful: rolling hills and little villages in each valley. We were still in the Bourgogne (Burgundy) area, which is primarily agricultural, mostly grapes. The Canal de Centre weaves its way along the side of hills with the highway on the downhill side. We met two oncoming péniche that day, which was quite a challenge. The canal was very narrow, so just the slightest drift off the fairway would have us run aground.

The little villages along the way looked ancient and were neat as a pin. The homes were of old stone construction, with clay tile roofs all drooping and sagging but with stunning oak doors and window shutters. All the bridges and locks were decorated with potted flowers. After twenty-nine locks, we tied up late afternoon in Chagny, Saône-et-Loire, which is famous for its food. From where we were tied up, we could see charcuteries and patisseries with sumptuous displays in their windows, so we knew where to get our croissants for breakfast the next morning. Pat was not feeling well. Apart from suffering a bit from a cold, she was feeling overworked and depressed. It had been a tough day as we had done twenty-nine locks. The girls were bothering her. I was bothering her. She decided to go for a walk after dinner by herself. When she returned, she went straight to bed.

Things were better for her the next morning, and we departed around 0800 hours for Chalon-sur-Saône in pouring rain. After going through twelve locks, we arrived around noon. The area was heavily industrialized and dirty. We passed a huge Kodak plant beside the river that had a rushing current. Logs and branches were drifting quickly and smashing into us. We finally fetched a marina or *Port de Plaisance* as it was called, and tied to a dock. Because the river was flooding, we had to inflate the dinghy to get ashore. This was going to be a stopover for a day or two, as we expected our friends would catch up to us. It was the next day when they started to arrive, and one by one they came until we were all assembled. The water level was increasing at the rate of one inch per hour, and by 2300 hours, a log smashed into and broke the dock we were all tied up to. We all scurried around in the dark and moved the three boats to a safer dock.

Péniche waits for us to finish our lock

The trip to Saint-Jean-de-Losne was uninteresting. All we could see was water, and all the fields bordering the canal were flooded. With no markers indicating where the canal was, we just had to guess using field fence posts as a guide when there were any. It was unnerving to see cattle standing ankle deep in water in what could have been the canal but of course was just on the edge. The current was so strong we were only able to advance at a little over a knot.

We had planned to meet Larry and Barry aboard *Wild Sage* in Saint-Jean-de-Losne and from there follow the canals to Basel, which shares a border with France, Germany, and Switzerland. They were already there waiting for us. We had a great reunion and heard all about their trip to Maine, west of Paris. They had been in Saint-Jean-de-Losne for the last couple of days and had heard that the canals were flooded and dangerous. We changed our plans deciding to continue to Dijon then take the train to Basel from there. I had more boat repairs to contend with. Air was still getting into the fuel injector pump. I couldn't see any air in the fuel line, so concluded that it was must be the fuel pump diaphragm. I could do no more than take it apart and put it back together and hope. I also replaced a length of the fuel line. There was always something to do. Also the refrigerator had stopped refrigerating. I checked for gas leaks and reconnected the ground wire but to no avail. Pat was losing confidence in my abilities, but I convinced her that it was cold enough so the refrigerator wasn't that necessary. She was concerned, however, that it might be a necessity once we reached the tropics, to which I responded that we were a long way off and that (maybe) I would have it fixed by that time.

Next morning the push was on; we both left early, and it rained all day. There was always a lock in view. We did twenty-three locks in only eighteen miles before we reached Dijon. There we tied up to a pontoon in a park area where we moored for five days. Dijon is known for its mustard, and we were surprised to hear that 90% of the mustard seed is imported from Canada. With my interest in car racing, I knew that the French Grand Prix was held in Dijon but not while we were there. We met three holidaymakers on a rental boat from Liechtenstein, a small country of only one hundred square miles between Switzerland and Austria. It is an extremely wealthy country, relying on taxes from heavy industry to provide its wealth. In fact, citizens don't have to pay personal income tax. Labour for the industry is primarily from Italy. It is mostly recognized throughout the world for Hilti Tools, used in the construction indus-try. From Dijon, we took the train to Beaune, known as the Capital of Burgundy Wines. Due to health reasons I don't drink alcohol, so I watched as they tasted the wine at Patriarche Wines, known for Kriter Brut Rose, a favourite. People were particularly surprised that I went through France and never had a drop of wine. I enjoyed going to the wineries for wine tasting but was quite happy to enjoy the festivities with a glass of water. I was always the designated walker, to get us back to the boat.

Apart from the wine, Beaune exhibits architectural features from pre-Roman and Roman eras. The roofs were glazed in terracotta green, yellow and black and arranged in geometric patterns. On the train coming back to our boat, we met a girl from Montana who was living with a French family for two months while on an exchange program. She was comfortable enough with her French that she spent all her spare time travelling the surrounding area, which must have been a wonderful experience for her.

Realizing that our hopes were dashed for visiting Switzerland, we left early morning to return to Saint-Jean-de-Losne. It rained all day again. The trip was a little more pleasant because the current was in our favour, but we still had to negotiate the same twenty-three locks. It was more time-consuming because we had to fill the locks before entering them this time as we were downhill going up.

When we arrived in Saint-Jean-de-Losne, we discovered that the water level had dropped about eighteen inches over the last six days. Wild Sage arrived the next day, and we prepared for the journey to Mâcon. The current in the Saone was in our favour. We knew it was going to take two days, so after only three locks and thirty-five miles, we tied up against the canal wall with only a bow line because the current was so strong it kept us hard against the wall. Even at rest, the knot meter was showing half to three quarters of a knot.

Carrying on the next day, we stopped in Tournus just to visit St. Philibert's Church, one of the oldest abbeys in France, built in the year 600. After lunch we got under way, fetching Mâcon at 1730 hours after thirty-eight miles and no locks. The city dock didn't look that great because of the current, so we searched out the local Port de Plaisance, which proved much more satisfactory.

Mâcon began as a river port in the 1st century BC inhabited by the Celts. It was known then as Matisco. During our walk, we passed Maison de Bois (house of wood), built in the 15th century and now a restaurant with beautifully carved wood on the entrance; then La Vieux Saint-Vincent Cathedral, originally from the 11th century but later rebuilt in 1808. As we walked along the river bank, we saw lots of rowers, apparently a major sport here. Pat and I walked over to the *gare* (station) to get information on trains to Geneva while the girls went grocery shopping for us. On their way out of the store, a rude attendant searched their grocery bags, accusing them of theft even though they had the receipt. Julie was very upset, and I can't say I blame her.

The next morning, Pat and I walked into town to buy tickets for the TGV (*Ligne à Grande Vitesse*, high-speed line) for Geneva. Larry and Barry had decided to stay behind. We had to pay full fare for the kids, not the half fare that we had been told the day before. The train left from eight kilometers away, so we took a bus to the train station. It was a fast and smooth train ride and wonderful scenery going through the Jura mountain range.

We arrived in Geneva by lunch time. *Wow! What a magnificent city!* As early as 1291, the foundation of the Swiss Confederation ensured peace on the important mountain trade routes and was instrumental in Switzerland maintaining neutrality throughout the ages. Next was Switzerland's role in the Reformation in the 16th century, when the Protestants broke away from the Roman Catholic Church. We visited the University of Geneva, which features the Monument International de la Réformation, usually known as the Reformation Wall, depicting Calvinism supporters, with statues of William Farel, John Calvin, Theodore Beza, and John Knox. Next we saw the Hotel de Ville where the Geneva Convention was signed in 1864. We walked the cobblestone streets which were graced by magnificent old buildings like the St. Pierre Cathedral, from the 12th century, best-known as the home church of John Calvin. We visited the Musée de l'Horlogerie à Genève (clock museum). Of the many timepieces displayed, the one that impressed me the most was a huge one made out of wood.

We picnicked at Île Rousseau, a park on an island in the Rhone named after philosopher Jean-Jacques Rousseau. It was a beautiful setting with people feeding pigeons, ducks, and swans. Another park we encountered had a bathroom area for dogs identified with a picture of a St. Bernard in the sand. We walked to Brunswick Monument commemorating the life of Charles II, Duke of Windsor 1804–1873. He left his fortune to Geneva to erect a tomb modeled after the Scaliger tombs in Verona, Italy.

All good things come to an end. In the evening, we boarded the train back to Mâcon. On our walk back to *Melissa II,* we found the water had risen even higher than when we left.

Two days later, we departed with the current in our favour, averaging 7 knots with a boost from the Saône River. We arrived at Collonges-au-Mont-d'Or mid-afternoon but walked back to Rochetaillée-sur-Saône for the Auto Museum (Musée de l'Automobile Henri Malartre) in a magnificent castle built in 1173 with a colourful tile roof. Among the cars displayed that were of particular interest to me were a 1918 Morgan, a McLaren that Bruce McLaren drove to victory in the 1968 Canadian Grand Prix (where I was in the supporting races), and a 1960 Cooper Climax Formula One car.

The next morning we had breakfast and then took the bus into Lyon. The city was impressive, boasting ancient churches and buildings. We walked along the Rhône taking in many of the sights before hiking up the hill to Théâtres

Romains de Fourvière in a park south of the Notre-Dame de Fourvière Basilica. This open-air theatre built 17 BC is still in use today. The Basilica of Notre-Dame de Fourvière, was gorgeously ornate with ceramic tile murals gracing the walls. When we bused back to the boat, it had become quite chilly and we couldn't use the heater because we were out of kerosene.

Once we left Lyon, we were getting a terrific boost from the Rivière Rhône. In fact, we were averaging over 10 knots for the next sixty miles in spite of negotiating four locks, one of which had a drop of fifty feet. A lock keeper greeted us yelling, "Hello, Canada," and we engaged in conversation about our trip. By late afternoon, we fetched Tournon-sur-Rhône where we again met Mark, a young Englishman bound for Africa aboard his twenty-five-foot sloop with an outboard motor. He was having a terrible time with the engine because it was not running very well. I loaned him our dinghy motor, a 15-horsepower Evenrude, arranging to meet in Sète to get it back. It was the town that culminated the canal/river passage to the Mediterranean and was now only a few days away.

From there, the run down the Rhône was breathtaking! There were high rocky cliffs with ruins of ancient castles on both sides. We estimated that the current was 6 knots, caused by the flooding, giving us a boat speed of 12 knots. It was uncomfortably fast because we had to keep the engine running at full speed to maintain steering. We had one scary moment when a fellow boater screamed at me, warning me of an old submerged bridge abutment that was dead ahead of us. I hadn't seen it so I gave full rudder, and we barely missed it, clearing our stern by a boat length. It made my knees shake for many days after. In fact, it still haunts me today. We were heading straight for it, and it would have sunk the boat. My thought of fighting for survival in a river running 6 knots was not a pleasant one. Pat saw what we had escaped, but we didn't talk about it. I brushed it off as if it was no problem.

After five locks, one of which had a drop of seventy feet, we fetched Saint-Étienne-des-Sorts. We tied to bollards by a staircase that led up to the town. The setting was fantastic. It was like being in a huge amphitheatre. Castles in all directions surrounded us. Fortunately, we were able to get kerosene for our heater. It was getting really cold, so we fired it up immediately and made *Melissa II* warm and cozy for the evening.

The following morning was quite chilly, with a strong mistral (cold, dry strong winds across the mountains) from the north. Again, it was ancient castles on every peak. We did three locks, one of which took us ninety minutes, before we fetched Arles early afternoon. We tied up against the river wall just south of remains of an ancient viaduct, Aqueduct of Arles at Barbegal. I found it so fascinating walking to be walking the streets that dated back to Roman times.

It was November 10, 1981. We departed Arles about noon after a walk about town. We were going against the current before we reached the Petit-Rhône, then there was little current and the canal was quite narrow. This area is called Camargue and is home to the Camargue wild horses. We saw many horses and pink flamingos along our way through flat low-lying swampy land that was rather dull.

We eventually got to our last lock. Imagine! We had transversed 232 locks; 160 of them we had operated ourselves, 31 were electric, and 41 were automatic. Now we were on the Canal du Rhône à Sète on the home stretch to the Mediterranean. We reached Aigues-Mortes, a small town of about 5,000 people that is famous for its ramparts completely enclosing the town. Founded during Louis IX's reign, it used to be a seaport but now is five miles from the Mediterranean. The water has receded that much. Salt production from the flats has been the main industry since the 8th century.

The next day was Remembrance Day. All through France, we had been discussing the impact of the world wars with Julie and Jennifer. It is hard to imagine that the death rate in the World War I was sixteen million, and over sixty million people were killed in World War II. I had been reminded of it all the way through France.

Having spent almost three months in France, our next destination was Sète. From now on the canal was straight and featureless. When we reached Frontignan, we had to wait three hours before the drawbridge opened to let us through. We found the town heavily industrialized and dirty. Some boys along the shore threw rocks at us. Needless to say, Frontignan was not our favourite place in France.

We passed under the bridge at 1700 hours and pushed on to Sète. It was dark when we got to a railway bridge that looked extremely low, but fellow boaters assured us we could pass under it, which we did with about six inches to spare. We rafted to *Nordlys*, ending our trip through the inland waterways of France. It was a pleasant evening of relaying our experiences and listening to theirs. We learned where we could erect our mast at no cost and prepare for our journey in the Mediterranean.

While spending the next week waiting for Mark to arrive with our outboard motor, I used the time to repair sails and do boat maintenance, an ongoing challenge. We enjoyed lots of socializing as there were many boaters in the harbour, and each had their own story to tell.

None had children with them, and I felt badly that the girls didn't have playmates. In fact, most of our way through France had been without many children their age for them to socialize with. They did receive lots of attention from the adults we met, but it wasn't the same.

It was a treat to have nice warm showers. We did laundry, got the mast up and rigged, picked up our mail from the Port Authority, did a big grocery shopping and topped up our wine supply. We learned early in our travels of France that the best and cheapest way to get the local regional wines was to visit wine kiosks and fill your own container. We used a 1.5 litre plastic container and referred to our wine as "Château Plastique." We obtained charts for the coast from Italy to Gibraltar. Each evening was socializing, eating too much and going to bed too late, but it was fun.

Larry, Barrie, and Mark arrived late in the evening of November 17. There was lots of storytelling. Then it was time for us to depart. Our plan was to proceed east to Italy, but from there we weren't sure. We had been hearing that winter was not a good time to sail in the Mediterranean, mainly because of the mistrals, with winds coming from the north-west that reach speeds up to 50 knots. In fact, a few weeks later, we heard that Mark had lost his boat in a storm, but thankfully he was rescued.

CHAPTER 11

The Evil Mediterranean

"Being hove to in a long gale is the most boring way of being terrified I know."

– Donald Hamilton

We had three bridges to pass under before we reached the open sea. All our fellow boaters were on deck blasting their horns giving us a send-off. Steve and Jackie left the same time but in the opposite direction towards the Straits of Gibraltar. We hadn't decided if we were going to sail through the night or stop and anchor. We had numerous sail changes ranging from double-reefed main and a lapper to no wind at all and motoring. It was cold so we fetched anchorage in Golfe des Saintes-Maries, which was an open roadstead. That meant we had to be very conscious of winds coming up during the night. It was rocky all night, and Julie was suffering from a severe cold so we kept the heater going.

The next morning, we headed to Marseille with the winds in our teeth. It was hopeless tacking back and forth, so we motor sailed most of the way, fetching the harbour at 1600 hours and tying up at the costly CNL dock. It is really posh, and we were the smallest boat there. Julie was nursing her cold, so Jennifer came with us as we strolled in shoulder-to-shoulder traffic along the famous Canebière Street. Marseille is next to Paris in size and is the oldest city in France, having been inhabited since 600 BC. We made the long climb up to the Notre-Dame de la Garde. The basilica had magnificent bright-coloured ceramic tile with gorgeous paintings on the walls. The crypt, built in 1242, is used mainly for confessions. Sailors have been coming here over the centuries, praying for guidance and safe passages for their voyages. It added a personal touch for us. There is a beautiful gold statue of the Virgin Mary holding Jesus in outstretched arms with one pointing to the sea and the other inland. As with many buildings in France, there were canon holes from the Second World War on the walls. It would have been a breathtaking view from the top, but it was so smoggy, we couldn't see our boat down below in the harbour.

After walking around the port looking at the fishing boats and fish market, we went for lunch. Marseille is famous for bouillabaisse, a stew made with fresh fish, crabs, mussels and a host of other sea life. Restaurants had people on the street herding tourists into their restaurants for their bouillabaisse. We succumbed to the temptation, and it was very good but poked a sizable hole in our budget.

We departed mid-afternoon, going around the Frioul Archipelago, which comprises four islands, one of which is the location of Château d'If. Originally built as a fortress to defend Marseille in the early 1500s, it was later used as the most feared prison in France. No one actually escaped from it, although in Alexandre Dumas' novel, *The Count of Monte Cristo*, an escape was successful. Today, it is a tourist attraction similar to Alcatraz in San Francisco. We fetched Port-Miou, which is not a town but three fiords surrounded by steep bald rock face. There was evidence of old fortresses everywhere we looked. We used a stern line attaching it to a ring embedded in the rock wall for that purpose, to stop from swinging around. In the evening, while the girls did school work, we studied charts and updated our log. The sound of the waves breaking on the cliff ten feet away all night long was very unnerving.

Pill boxes from WWII were visible on the cliffs

It was dark the next morning when we weighed anchor. It was flat calm but overcast all day. We anchored for the night at Île de Bagau, one of a group of rocky islands. There were castles on every mountain top. We would have had to blow up the dinghy to go ashore to look around so we didn't bother; instead, the girls made dinner, while I wrote my magazine articles and Pat made a courtesy flag for Monaco. We had yards of colourful spinnaker cloth on board, which she used for making flags for all the countries we visited. It is a courtesy to fly the country ensign on the starboard spreader. We would also be compelled to fly a yellow quarantine flag when entering a foreign country to alert customs and immigration authorities that we hadn't cleared for entrance.

We got another early start and were blessed with a following wind for a change. We had a pleasant day sailing in bright clear skies. I saw a sunfish but didn't really know what it was. I was shocked to see such a large fish head with hardly any body behind it. It had a dorsal fin like a shark. It wasn't until I described it to a fisherman that I learned that it was a sunfish.

We came into the lee of Île Sainte-Marguerite, the largest island of the Lérins Islands, about half a mile offshore from Cannes on the Riviera. We tied up at the dock and an older French couple came over to chat. It was strenuous, but my French was improving so we had a nice visit. We walked up to Fort Royal, the château fort. Along the path, there were beautiful cacti growing. The island was first inhabited during Roman times, but it wasn't until the late 1600s that the fort was converted to a fortress prison where the Man in the Iron Mask, believed to be the older brother of Louis XIV, was held captive. There are many theories about his identity. My favourite is Voltaire's rendition, that he was the older illegitimate brother of Louis XIV, thus in line to inherit the throne. Because Louis XIV wanted the throne, he had his brother held captive in an iron mask, eliminating any chance of recognition, and he went on to be king.

The extremely strong winds that had occurred throughout the night had subsided when we departed for Monaco early the next morning. We arrived early afternoon tying up, stern to (Mediterranean style) as per the wharfinger's instructions, alongside a huge boat registered in Kuwait with an American crew from San Diego. They were great neighbours and gave us lots of tips on what to see and do. There was no question that, of the dozens of boats tied up, we were the smallest. The largest was *Atlantis II*, just less than 400 feet long, owned by a Greek shipping magnate. Our docking charge for four days stay was a mere $40.

It is surprising that Monaco has become such a focal point. There is no natural harbour; the shoreline is all steep cliffs, and building costs must be atrocious because it is solid rock, yet it is the most densely populated country in the world. Monte Carlo, the wealthiest quarter, is where most of the action is. This world-renowned tourist and recreation centre for the rich and famous has the highest number of millionaires and billionaires per capita in the world. The streets are full of Ferraris, Lamborghinis, Maseratis, Porches, Rolls, and Bentleys. Apart from the famous Casino, Monaco has hosted the most prestigious automobile race in the world – the annual Grand Prix de Monaco Formula One – since 1950. Its course is through the streets of town and is scheduled usually in late May, but preparations begin three months earlier. Also, the Monte Carlo Rally, which has been held since 1911, has long been considered to be one of the toughest events in rallying. The town is thought to have been discovered by Hercules, who it is believed to have lived there around 1250 BC.

We walked the streets used for the Formula One race. It had sharp corners through town and passed the Casino with a fast downhill stretch before the viaduct. Having seen the races televised since the late 50s, I was familiar with most of the track. Just exiting the viaduct – in 1967 – in second place in his Ferrari, Lorenzo Bandini had a horrific accident that took his life. I had seen it all on television, and the memory is still vivid in my mind. It had been a hay bale that Bandini struck, sending him into the air then bursting into flames upon landing. As a result of that event, hay bales were no longer used as barricades on race tracks. Back in the sixties, the fatalities in car racing were numerous. Thank goodness for the safety changes now imposed on drivers, cars and racetracks. When I started racing in 1964, I wore shorts and a tee-shirt. It wasn't long before Nomex fireproof clothing had to be worn. At my home track – Mosport Park – a driver was killed every year in my seven years racing there.

We visited the Prince's Palace of Monaco, built in 1171, to see the changing of the guards. It is perched high up on a hill, and the walkway down to town was in beautiful mosaic tile. The girls had a wonderful time in the amusement area. Because it was Wednesday, the schools were closed so there were lots of other children to play with. At that age, language is not a problem.

We chanced upon a shop specializing in models and bought a model of a Morgan that I still have with my number 186 painted on it. The friendly proprietor told us of model car races that followed a circuit around the swimming pool near the harbour. Just west of the main harbour is a smaller one, Port de Fontvieille, where we met Linda and Harvey from California aboard *Zest,* a fifty-foot wooden boat that they had been working on for four years.

Once back to *Melissa II* in the main harbour, we met Mike Healey, who was the agent for Admiralty Charts. Over a glass of wine we learned more about Monaco and surrounding areas, and he suggested Menton as our next stop, albeit we were reluctant to depart at this time.

Menton was only five miles away. Reputedly the warmest winter resort on the French Rivera's Côte d'Azur, it had been frequented by the English since Queen Victoria went there. The harbour was crowded, but we managed to "stern to" at the quay. The winds howled all night, shifting our bow anchor about five feet.

We headed for Bordighera, Italy, a charming medieval town. We checked in with the port captain who filled out reams of paperwork, allowing us to tour Italian waters for a year. We went to the bank to exchange francs for lira, which also required paperwork that took over an hour. With France being right next door, one would expect that the exchange would be familiar to them. We strolled for most of the day in town and walked the country roads amongst palatial estates with beautiful gardens terraced down to the sea.

We had discussed going further east and through the Suez Canal and complete a trip around the world, but I was nervous about that route, having heard many tales about piracy. With three blond girls aboard, it seemed a little risky. We decided to forgo the rest of Italy, departing at midnight going west. We were on our way home now. Our planned route was to head for the Straits of Gibraltar then down the African coast.

After two hours of gentle winds, they really burst forth, an amazing switch from calm to force 11 in a matter of minutes. I was on deck all night making sail changes from trysail to full main and genoa repeatedly. It was exhausting, so we finally altered course for Nice, arriving and tying up to a pontoon in the early morning and going to sleep. We were visited by the Port Captain who was annoyed that we hadn't checked in but warmed up quickly and invited us to his office to get weather predictions for all along the coast. He was very helpful and suggested we sneak along the shore and advised us of safe spots to head for when the mistrals came up. These strong cold and north-westerly winds blow from southern France into the Gulf of Lion in the northern Mediterranean,

We departed late afternoon, and within an hour, winds grew to gale force. We ducked into Antibes, tying up to the gas dock. This historic town was founded in the 5th century BC and has been an important port ever since. It is drenched in history, but we just weren't in the mood for searching it out.

We departed Antibes early morning and didn't really know our next stop. It was going to depend on the wind. We had favourable conditions most of the day. At night we began to see a confusion of lights offshore, red flares being fired at regular intervals of a minute. Then we saw what looked like a large well-lit drilling barge giving off a signal in Morse code, dit dit dah, the letter U that signals a sandbar or rocks ahead. It was all very confusing until we realized that we were close to the French Naval base at Toulon, so we went in the harbour and tied up at the gas dock. Our progress had been good, having got a boost from the current. It was late at night, and I had to climb the mast to retrieve a jib halyard.

One thing that we were learning about the Mediterranean was that winter time is not a good time for cruising. The winds go from virtually none to howling gales in a matter of minutes. Generally, the seas are choppy but don't get to any height because we are close to a windward shore; the wind, mostly the mistrals, blow from the north. We experienced similar conditions later when sailing down the African shore, although the winds were from the east over the Sahara.

There were lots of ships going in and out the harbour the next morning, which made us realize how large this naval base was. Usually when we encountered a naval vessel at sea, we would dip our flag as a courtesy, but with so many ships, we just waved. We experienced typical Mediterranean sail-damaging conditions, with the sail tearing under the first reefing point. I couldn't react fast enough to avoid it. The wind went from a soft breeze to force 6 in a matter of minutes. Then, after only an hour, we were back to gentle sailing with the wind from the north. That didn't last long when it swung around coming from the west, the direction we were headed. We resorted to motoring but decided to put into Île Ratonneau, in the Frioul Archipelago, when the seas started to build and winds climbed to force 6 quickly. It was an indication to us that "all hell could break loose", and it did. Caesar used to hang out here in 49 BC when the Roman fleet besieged Marseilles. I wonder what weather conditions they experienced? The island was deserted except that the City of Marseilles was building a marina with habitat housing that had been under construction for six years. Nobody was there that day, probably because of the weather. Signs advertised units for sale for $15,000 US.

It was December 4, 1981. Pat and I discussed our intentions, and decided we wanted to get to Barcelona for Christmas. Our next safe port was Port de Carro, which was only twelve miles away.

We departed at noon as the winds had dropped to force 7. *What was I thinking?* I felt that we would be on a reach with the wind on our starboard. We could proceed along the shore that sheltered us from the waves, allowing us to reach Carro easily. We were under double-reefed main and storm jib when we were suddenly hit with force 11 winds. I got the main down, but even with the storm jib, we were pegging the knot meter at 12 knots and heeled so far over that water came over the combing, flooding the cockpit. I changed course to get back to the harbour we had just left. As we cleared the point, I hanked on the trysail in an effort to go to weather, then fired up the motor, desperately trying to make the harbour entrance. It was nip and tuck clearing the very narrow entrance with rocky shore on both sides. We made it and headed for the dock. Our bow hit the dock with such force that an eyebolt poked a hole in the hull about two feet above the waterline. I tied off the bow with two lines and then two spring lines and a stern line. Once secured, the four of us went for a walk to loosen up and get some exercise. The wind howled all night with such force that we were listing hard against the dock.

The next morning, Pat and I decided to search out the weather station at the top of the hill of solid rock. We climbed up the hill, but the wind was so strong, Pat couldn't go any farther. I continued but crawled on my hands and knees for the last hundred feet. It startled the two men inside when I opened the door. They were very helpful and told me the winds were going to continue strong and I should just stay tied up at the marina. While I was there, the anemometer was reading 50 knots gusting to 70 knots. That's hurricane force, and was not encouraging. When I left, they strung a rope out for me to hold onto to go down the hill. Back at *Melissa II,* we socialized with a French couple on a thirty-eight-foot home-built boat. They thought we were crazy to have set out, but we knew that already. My anemometer didn't fall below 50 knots all day. While waiting two days for the winds to drop to a reasonable level, the girls did school work, I sewed the foot of the main, which had ripped during our attempted escape, and Pat sewed up a Spanish courtesy flag.

Winds subsided during the night. We thought we had better take advantage of it, so we left for Carro, which was only two hours away. It was a nice comfortable sail comparatively speaking, but we did manage to tear the tack on our 150% genoa. We rafted to a steel French boat and ended up staying an extra day, only because it was headwinds and rough seas, however, by this time we were all getting bored and fed up.

Things didn't improve the next day, but foolishly we decided to make a run for it. We ran into headwinds and rough seas that not only slowed us but brought us to a dead stop. We headed back to Carro again. We listened to every weather forecast throughout the day and even set the alarm to listen to them during the night. It howled all night, bashing us against the French boat we were rafted to. By 0530 hours, the wind slowed and fishing boats were leaving the harbour. We joined them. They had a pretty good sense of local weather conditions. If they were going out to drag fish nets, it would be safe for us go out too.

It was not a pleasant day, but we persevered, tacking into head winds, motor sailing . . . anything to keep us moving. By 1730 hours, we made Sète, where we had left from almost a month earlier. After the long day, we had only gone sixty-two miles. We did a layover because we were exhausted and needed a rest and some conventional meals. It blew all night, but we departed at 0830 hours in strong winds from the south-west. We motor sailed and tacked with just the main to make headway. Later in the afternoon, the winds subsided, but the seas were uncomfortably rough. At 2000 hours, a military launch hailed us to heave to. They asked where we were coming from. They were courteous and guessed that we probably were not carrying any drugs, so they let us carry on, recommending Port Vendes for a comfortable stopover. When we fetched the harbour, low and behold, there was *Wild Sage*. Even though it was past bedtime, we stayed up talking about our adventures. We heard that the crew of a Morgan Out Island 41 had trouble when their self-furling jib came unfurled and they had to be taken off by a rescue boat. The boat was later recovered by the Italian navy and graciously returned to the owners.

We lounged around in the morning, leaving after lunch in light winds from the east. *Wild Sage* left with us. The swells that had built up over the last few days were very uncomfortable. After a couple of hours, *Wild Sage* turned back as the swells were really bothering them and the wind had picked up and was in our teeth. We carried on to the fishing port of El Port de la Selva, our first in

Spain. It was Sunday, so everything was closed. At the police station, we asked about customs and immigration. Their advice was not to worry about it and to check in at Barcelona.

We departed at 0930 hours the next day, not knowing what to expect from the weather. Wind was from the north and moderate, but the skies looked ominous. A fisherman motored over to warn us of a tramontane, a strong, dry cold wind from the north. Also, an aircraft swooped over us almost at mast height on three occasions, so we thought it might be in our best interests to seek the nearest port. We headed for a breakwater, but the entrance had breaking waves across it, so we headed back out to sea. Just as we did, the winds started to scream. We set the trysail and reached along close to shore, making for Palamós only nine miles away. Even with the wind coming off the shore, the waves grew to enormous heights, steep and close together. By the time we got to the harbour entrance, the wind miraculously stopped. It was about 1800 hours when we tied up to the gas dock and Pat spoke her first Spanish: "Puesto por esta noches?" Neither of us nor the person she asked knew what it meant, but it had a nice ring to it. I think she wanted to know how much it cost for the night.

When we departed at 0700 hours, it was still dark and the seas were sloppy. Early afternoon, we were abeam of Blanes, the end of the Costa Brava that stretches from Blanes to the French border. Since the winds had turned against us and we were making very little headway, we came back to Blanes, taking up the last spot at the dock. Later, an Australian fifty-two-foot boat, *Bimbimbi*, with Jamie and Katrina, arrived. Jamie had built the boat himself out of ferrocement. I moved out so they could tie up at the dock then we rafted to them. It certainly made more sense than having a huge boat rafted up to us. That evening we enjoyed getting to know each other. They were completing their circumnavigation to Australia and were headed for the Panama Canal as we were, so we expected to see a lot of them en route.

When we left in the dark next morning, they were just ahead of us. Winds were strong at the onset. We started with a double reef in the main but soon had to put up the trysail, arriving at Barcelona at 1530 hours behind *Bimbimbi*. We were pleasantly surprised to find *Nordlys* there and had a great reunion with Ed and Nancy. We all decided to stay a couple of weeks and spend Christmas in Barcelona. Our only commitment was to be in Almerimar by December 30 to pick up my niece Megan who was flying from Ontario to join us there.

In the morning, Pat and I went to the information centre and got the name of a dentist and a doctor. Pat was having a tooth problem, and I was suffering from a sore shoulder, which was not surprising, considering all the sails I had been hauling down. The dentist was very helpful; diagnosing that Pat's uneven teeth were causing a bite problem, he filed off a little, which did the trick. Later that day I saw the doctor who had spent four years in Chicago, so spoke perfect English. He diagnosed bursitis or tennis elbow and also detected that I had a hyper-active problem, which didn't surprise Pat at all.

Barcelona was founded in Roman times and has been besieged several times during its history. We walked Las Ramblas, the famous promenade from the port to the town centre. In front of the Catedral de la Santa Cruz y Santa Eulalia, known as the Barcelona Cathedral, hundreds of booths sold Christmas decorations, nativity scenes, books, candles and figurines. The Cathedral, built in the 13th century, was beautifully decorated in a Christmassy fashion. The exterior stone work was magnificent with exquisite gargoyles. A short distance away is the Basílica i Temple Expiatori de la Sagrada Família, designed by Antoni Gaudi. You wouldn't consider it a classical design, but in a whimsical way, it was magnificent. You can see where the expression using his name came from, or at least that is what I thought. It was gaudy all right! We certainly picked the perfect place to celebrate Christmas. The maritime museum, at the end of the promenade, has a life-size replica of *La Real*, the largest galleon of its time and the flagship of Don Juan de Austria in the Battle of Lepanto in 1571. At the time, it was the largest battle between galleys in history, in which a fleet of the Holy League, an alliance of Christian powers of the Mediterranean, decisively defeated the Ottoman.

Back at *Melissa II*, we caught up on boat maintenance. Our Canadian flag often attracted passersby who were curious about us. Then to our surprise, Larry and Barry showed up but not in their boat. They had come by train and told us the horrible story of running onto a beach that they mistook as the entrance to a harbour. *Wild Sage* suffered severe damage, and Larry suffered broken ribs. A Spanish man and his American wife took them in. The boat was high and dry up on a beach, and a channel would have to be dredged to retrieve it. Then it would be taken to El Masnou, just east of Barcelona, to be hauled where repairs could be made.

Now it was Christmas! It was a beautiful sunny day. After a fried egg tbreak-fast, Pat put the stuffed turkey in the oven, and preparations began. We would be leaving the following day, so we spent much of our time saying goodbye to many of the people we had come to know during our stay; however, by the end of a long, exhausting day, we were tired and ready for bed.

At 0645 hours, we departed in light winds from the north-west; it was chilly although sunny for most of the day. *Bimbimbi* was just behind us. It was a relief that the weather wasn't threatening and after fifty 50 miles, we fetched Tarragona. Legend has it that it was founded 2000 BC. Then, according to the information centre, Augustus, founder of the Roman Empire, wintered here after his Cantabrian campaign and bestowed many marks of honour on the city. Augustus formed a triumvirate with Mark Antony and Marcus Lepidus to defeat the assassins of Caesar, so this would have been just after 44 BC.

After dinner we all went for a walk on a walkway along a steep cliff overlook-ing the sea, eventually leading to the old town wall. The Cathedral of Tarragona was more striking than the Barcelona Cathedral.

We were confident we could make Castellón de la Plana next, but it was ninety miles away and with the weather we had been experiencing, it could be more than a day. We departed ahead of *Bimbimbi* at 0800 hours in pouring rain. I spent much of the day dancing around the deck changing sails and getting drenched right through my rain gear. I hanked on every sail in the locker during the course of the day. Wind conditions varied from calm to force 7. By 2200 hours, seas were rough, and with the wind in our teeth, we were making little headway. *Bimbimbi* passed us as if we were standing still, which we were most of the time. We finally got in to Castellón at 0130 hours the next day just behind *Bimbimbi*. They got their main sheet wound around the prop. We were too beat to do anything about it that night, so we went to bed and tackled it the next morning, departing at 1000 hours.

It was another one of those days. The weather predicted force 11 all the way to the Azores. Just as we passed some fishing boats heading for shore, I went through some dramatic sail changes. I set the number 3 jib, but before getting back to the cockpit, I had to put another reef in the main; then, as I was tighten-ing the cunningham, the wind screamed, and I had to drop the main, putting up the trysail, then scurry forward to drop the number 3 and hank on the storm jib. We finally arrived at Javea exhausted, rafted up to *Bimbimbi* and went to bed.

After fuelling up, we departed to experience another scary day. This time it was waterspouts, something we hadn't experienced before and certainly would never want to be exposed to again. With a force 8 blowing, we stayed close to shore to avoid the sloppy seas. We were reaching under double reefed main. Once we rounded a point of land, the wind increased to force 9, and I hanked on the trysail. Suddenly, we could see a waterspout off to port; then another one and another one. They are tornados on the ocean and can be lethal if you get too close. People lined the shoreline watching us; we were the only two boats in sight.

We headed into Calpe harbour, tying up stern to the dock. *Bimbimbi* chose another dock, but later moved over to ours once the winds subsided.

The original plan was to sail to Alicante to pick up my niece Megan at the airport, but because of the dreadful wind conditions, we couldn't make it in time. Consequently, I took a bus into Alicante to meet her early the next morning. Back on *Melissa II*, Pat and the girls were excited to see her, as they hadn't seen her since her visit with us in the Virgin Islands. After dinner, we all walked along the promenade to town. Calpe is very touristy and is popular with the British and the Germans. Early Spanish history tells us it was first settled in the Bronze Age, 5,000 years ago. It has had quite a colourful history.

The next day, we prepared to welcome in 1982. It was New Year's Eve! We spent most of the day tuning our instruments, preparing for an evening of singsong. We celebrated on *Melissa II* with the *Bimbimbi* crew with pizza, Greek lasagna, salad, and a cake made by Jennifer. After dinner, out came my banjo, and we all burst into song, which went on well beyond midnight.

Happy New Year! The wind was howling from the west, just like last year, which was only yesterday. We left the dock mid-morning heading for Alicante. For most of the day – with winds in our teeth between force 6 and 8 – I was constantly changing sails until we reached our destination.

Bimbimbi had decided to sail on to Almerimar for boat repairs. We planned to pull into Cartagena, which was only sixty miles away, so we could cook our New Year's ham. We didn't arrive until 2100 hours, so it was an evening of cooking and eating. We didn't do our usual evening stroll but took time in the morning to do some shopping and get caught up on chores. We departed for Almerimar about noon, realizing we had an overnight sail ahead of us and it turned out to be just that. Megan and Julie did the night watch. I did some ham radio contacts with Rudy back at Flushing, England, and Bill in Florida. I had been having fairly regular contacts with them since we reached the Mediterranean.

Almerimar was appealing because it was a large yacht harbour with lots of facilities for boat repairs and a hoist for hauling, which we intended to use. We socialized with local harbour dwellers, while *Bimbimbi* was already on the hard when we arrived. Jamie was steam cleaning the hull while Katrina was in town shopping. Jamie gave us the news that it had not been working out with crew member Mark, so he had left. With just Jamie and Katrina aboard a fifty-two-foot schooner, it was a real handful.

On the hard in Almerimar, Spain

We got hauled, put on the hard and began work, cleaning the hull and waxing the top sides. It was a free bus ride to the nearest towns, El Ejido and Almeria, which we took advantage of. We had pleasant trips to town for shopping and ate *churros* for the first time. They are Spanish donuts that taste really scrumptious. We visited the Alcazaba, an 8th century Arab fortress, in a section of town that is typically Arabic, with small huts painted bright colours to ward off evil spirits. Housing continued up the mountain where people live in caves built into the rock face. When we got back to the harbour, *Nordlys* had arrived; it was amazing how cruisers kept running into each other.

January 7, 1982, we celebrated Jennifer's twelfth birthday, which began with her having breakfast and then opening presents. For dinner, *Melissa II* was down to her gunnels with guests for lasagna, garlic bread, and birthday cake. It was difficult to come out to the cockpit without engaging in conversation with someone. Also there were lots of round-table meetings with Jamie, Katrina, Ed, and Nancy regarding our route back to the Caribbean. We mulled over charts and decided to go to Casablanca, Canary Islands, then cross the Atlantic to Tobago.

We rented a little red Siat Panda, the Spanish rendition of the Italian Fiat. It was perfect for us to go on a beautiful drive through the Sierra Nevada Mountain range to reach Granada. Once there, we obtained a hotel room for the night and immediately started our tour. We visited Alhambra, which was constructed as a fortress in 889 and later converted into a royal palace.

The next day we headed 2,200 metres up the Sierra Nevada Mountains to the ski area. The girls were thrilled with the setting and had a wonderful time frolicking around in the snow. Finally, we left for home, the *Melissa II*. The drive was again beautiful, and we made stops to pick up fresh almonds and oranges right off the tree. When we arrived back at Almerimar, *Bimbimbi* was still on the hard. Fortunately you can still live on your boat when it is on the hard.

Malaga was eighty miles away, we planned to depart at 0400 hours. With no wind, we motored the whole day, getting a little boost from the current, arriving at 1800 hours. It is a huge commercial port but had few facilities for cruisers. The Club Nautico only accommodates twenty to thirty boats. We tied up outside of the Club quay the first night but were kicked off midday and had to move to the fishing quay. It was very dirty and smelly and a long walk to the port gate.

There were lots of forms to fill out for the officials. They said that someone had to be on board at all times. We hadn't run into that before. Every port in Spain had its own rules.

We stayed over for two days because there was so much to see. With a US aircraft carrier and another large naval ship anchored in the harbour, the town was crowded with sailors, much to the delight of the girls. We shopped at El Corte Ingles, a huge grocery and department store featuring dockside deliveries, which was great because we were so far from town. We toured the Alcazaba built in 1057 as a palace and fortress. The artesonado ceilings were magnificent. Ramparts connect it to the Gibralfaro way up on a ridge with fantastic views of the city. We walked through beautiful parks with date palms and orange trees lining the streets. The city was very impressive.

Back at the harbour, it was a different story. There appeared to be a lot of desperate people milling around the marina, although we tied up amongst the fishing boats and didn't feel threatened.

We departed early the next morning to our destination, Puerto José Banús. It was only thirty-two miles away, although it did take us seven hours through rough seas and headwinds. Being an adamant history buff, upon our arrival I began my investigation of Puerto José Banús by asking the wharfinger: "Who was José Banús?" The wharfinger said he had developed the luxury marina and shopping complex in 1970 and pointed out his house nearby. Well, so much for Spanish history. We had the usual reams of paperwork and had our passports stamped for the first time since entering Spain. Moorage was extremely reasonable at $4 per day. It's quite likely our fellow boaters were paying more as most of them were like ocean liners and manned by paid crew. The girls enjoyed browsing the dock front, lined with wall-to-wall boutiques and upscale restaurants. I enjoyed watching a girl arrive in a Rolls Royce, scantily clad in only a bikini bottom and high-heel shoes and walking a tiger. Under those conditions, it was hard to concentrate on boat chores, but I did get as far as changing the oil. The filter I had purchased in Barcelona was the wrong one, so I had to clean the old one with kerosene and replace it. Also, our mainsail was looking a little worse for wear with all our makeshift stitching, so I took it to a local sail maker who would have it finished in a few days when we returned with Megan. We all enjoyed having her travelling with us. We had made reservations for her to fly from Malaga, but we were going to continue along the coast with her as far as Gibraltar then return to Banús where I would take her by bus to Malaga for her flight.

In the early morning we departed Banús heading for Gibraltar, only thirty-two miles away. My first glimpse of the Rock sent shivers up my spine. I had read so much war history where Gibraltar had played a major part. There was no wind, which was fine because we had no sails. (Well, we did have jibs but no mainsail.) We motored into the harbour early afternoon and immediately fetched the dock across from *Nordlys*. Our purpose here was to take in the Autohelm (electric self-steering) and our EPERB (Emergency Position-Indicating Radio Beacon), which when activated produces, a signal alerting Search and Rescue of our location.

We docked alongside the airport, and it was quite a thrill to see a Harrier Jump Jet come in for a landing. It was amazing to watch! It made a quick pass over the airport, then came in and hovered for a few seconds before dropping down to the tarmac like a helicopter.

The girls went up the mountain to see the Gibraltar apes. Megan and Julie met a couple of American Navy cadets who took them out for a walk in the evening. Our plan was to go back to Banús to bus Megan to the Malaga airport. Because of boat chores, we didn't get away until mid-afternoon. It was perfect weather with moderate wind, so with just the lapper, no main, we were averaging 6.5 knots, arriving at Banús 1900 hours. It wasn't the easiest harbour to find in the dark. Although the chart indicated that the harbour light is visible for twelve miles, it was very dim and we almost missed it.

The next morning, Meg and I took the bus to Malaga for her flight home. We were going to miss her. We had such a good time with her and almost talked her into joining *Bimbimbi* as a crew member to cross the Atlantic, but she had other commitments.

We left Banús at 0600 hours in howling winds. We heard on the maritime network that a boat had sunk off Cadiz, but all on board were rescued by helicopter. We didn't hear any more details than that. It was back to Gibraltar in a roundabout way. We sailed to Algeciras, on the west side of the Bay of Gibraltar opposite Gibraltar. We had befriended a couple who lived in La Linea, which is immediately across two chain link fences from Gibraltar, but in 1982, you couldn't go from Gibraltar to Spain. Relations between Spain and Britain had always been a bit tenuous since 1713 when Gibraltar was ceded to Britain under the Treaty of Utrecht. Gibraltar has been occupied over the ages, from the Neanderthal period, through the Classical and on to the Moorish, Spanish, and now under British rule. Between the two fences was no man's land, with British armed guards on the Gibraltar side and Spanish armed guards on the La Linea side. It was supposed to be resolved in 1982, but the Falklands War had diverted Britain's attention so it didn't take place until 1985. As it turned out, we were so nervous about leaving our boat unattended in Algeciras that we never did go to visit our friends.

Back in Gibraltar, Jamie and Katrina arrived, and we all had our work cut out in preparation for our Atlantic crossing. We had to ensure that our self-steering, along with everything else, was in good operating condition. I hoisted Pat to the top of the mast to repair the wind indicator and check the strobe light, which we would operate whenever we encountered ocean traffic at night. Our Adler-Barbour refrigerator wasn't working, so we phoned them, arranging to have a module sent to the Canary Islands for us to pick up. Some of the windows were leaking as a result of the howling winds and spray we had encountered so I resealed them all. We allowed ourselves ten days so we had some sightseeing time and, of course, plenty of time for socializing in the evening. Julie went out the odd evening with Ed, her American Navy cadet friend. Jennifer joined them on occasion, and sometimes we all went to a movie.

There are over 150 caves in the rock of Gibraltar, including Saint Michael's cave, the most famous one. We were astonished at its size, which includes a huge auditorium staging symphony orchestra performances and seating for one hundred spectators. The Gibraltar apes are another attraction. When walking along the road, they would come and jump on us. Pat wasn't all that pleased when I asked her to not shoo one away that was sitting on her shoulder – picking away at her hair – so I could take a picture. *I got the picture!*

Gibraltar Ape on Pat's shoulder

We took a side trip to Ceuta to get some diesel fuel. Ceuta is a permanently inhabited Spanish territory in mainland Africa, directly across the straights from Gibraltar. It is only a little over seven miles, but tides create a tremendous current between the Atlantic and the Mediterranean. Unless you looked behind, you wouldn't realize how much you would have drifted on a crossing. In fact, during the World War II, German U-boats passed into the Mediterranean unde-tected with their motors off by waiting for an incoming tide.

Sail Inventory Course 101

In addition to a glossary of sailing terms, I thought it might help to explain what sails we used. A genoa is a staysail, headsail, or jib that overlaps the main mast. In our case we had:

- Number 1 – a jib that was 180% of the distance between the tack (lower corner of the sail's leading edge) on the bow and the mast.
- Number 2 – which was 150% of the distance.
- Number 3 – 110%, which is also called a lapper as it just overlaps the main mast.
- Storm sail – very small jib made of heavy canvas.
- Storm trysail – made of heavy canvas and replaces the function of the mainsail. It goes a fraction of the distance up the mast.
- Mainsail – attached to a boom and is hoisted up to the top of the mast. Ours had two reefing points that allowed us to reduce the sail area in heavy weather.
- Spinnaker – a large balloon-shaped sail often called a chute because it resembles a parachute. It has two sheets (lines at the lower corners of the sails): one running through a spinnaker pole running from the mast away to the side of the boat, the other running through a fairlead back to the winch. Spinnakers are made of light nylon cloth, often in bright colours. Can be used from a broad reach to a dead run.

CHAPTER 12

Preparing for Another Atlantic Crossing

"To reach a port we must set sail – Sail, not tie at anchor. Sail, not drift."

– Franklin D Roosevelt

It was 1830 hours before we left Gibraltar in strong winds. We were under storm jib and double-reefed main. Pat and I did the watch through the night as it was too rough for the girls. *Bimbimbi* left an hour after us with their new crew member, Tim, who was from England. By noon the next day, they passed us before we reached Cap Spartel, considered to be the entrance to the Strait of Gibraltar. Now although we had strong winds, the African coast protected us from the heavy seas. Once we rounded the Cap, we were far enough offshore that we could start our watch schedule with Julie and me doing the 2000 hours to 2400 hours. We were in radio contact with *Bimbimbi*, who was having trouble locating the entrance to Casablanca. This was because the light at Mohammedia just before Casablanca was easier to distinguish. It was 0600 hours and still dark when we entered the harbour and tied up to *Bimbimbi*.

After a couple of hours of sleep, we cleared with the authorities; however, because we had a gun on board, they took our passports, promising to return them at 1400 hours in three days when we planned to leave. They also implied that we should give them a souvenir at that time. Casablanca is the major port of North Africa and has a population in excess of three million. It is a fascinating city. We were hassled by shopkeepers and beggars on the streets. When we stopped for tea, we were surrounded by children who insisted on polishing our shoes.

We could hear recorded chants from the minarets indicating the time to pray. For three days, we browsed the Anfa, the original old quarters of Casablanca, and the Kasbah, the old walled fortified part of the city. Walking back to the boat, Tim and Julie lagged behind searching out souvenirs. On a quiet part of the street, a group of kids – likely in their preteens – pounced on them, grabbing at the shopping bags and Tim's camera. In the tussle, the camera landed on the pavement and broke.

When we returned to our boat, we waited for over an hour for the authorities to arrive with our passports. I was really annoyed and averted the issue about the souvenir for them, indicating that I couldn't get money without my passport. It was 1600 hours before we left in light air, in spite of threats from the weather department. We enjoyed a pleasant day sailing with full main and 180% genoa and even had eight hours with spinnaker. Jennifer was feeling unwell and couldn't keep anything down. It was quite likely something she ate.

We were back in touch with Ernie in Flushing and Bill in Florida by ham radio. We heard that a tanker had split in two and sank. Seventeen people were rescued by a Dutch helicopter, but sadly fifteen were lost. The storm was moving our way; swells were building and had an oily appearance, a harbinger to rough weather.

It took two days for it to strike, and then it was with fury. We kept in contact with *Bimbimbi*, who was having a rough time. She was taking green water over her bows that poured down through the hatch. With their bailing pump unable to keep up, they were bailing with buckets. We weren't having any problems at all. I'm a strong advocate of a boat our size because we just bobbed around like a cork on top of the waves. Large boats tend to bury their bows in the wave. I can recall a time when there was a storm and we were heading to Charleston, South Carolina, where a forty-one-foot sloop suffered damage and a crew member broke a rib. Jim Griffith, who was the captain on *Delfino II* (a motor launch over 200 feet long), was in fear of losing the boat. In essence, as long as you protect yourself from pitch polling by dragging something astern, you can weather severe storms.

Happy Valentine's Day! The storm had settled down quickly, and we were back to smooth sailing. Poor Jennifer had really suffered and wasn't in the mood for any celebration. When the sun came out, I was able to take sun shots during the day to confirm our dead reckoning. Pat and Julie took sights as well for practice, a good precaution in case I became incapacitated. We showered every day or two, naturally in salt water, and we used Joy dish soap, the only soap that foams in salt water. Through the canals of France, we lavished in warm fresh water at the marinas, but those days were now behind us.

It was another day before we reached Lanzarote, a Spanish archipelago and the most easterly island of the Canary Islands. The name Canary Islands has nothing to do with the canary bird but in fact gets its name from the wild dogs, canines that used to inhabit the islands. Since it was dark when we arrived, we had trouble locating the entrance to Arrecife, which is a major port on the isle of Lanzarote.

We hove to until daylight, then worked our way into the harbour and rafted up to *Bimbimbi*. The Customs official was a real character. He cleared *Bimbimbi* first; in fact, he cleared them of three bottles of beer, then came over to our boat and drank a bottle of wine. He proved to be lots of fun, and told us he had a four-month-old daughter named Jennifer, which put him in our Jennifer's good books.

The next morning we picked up a rental Daihatsu, a jeep-like vehicle that – with the top off – was more than accommodating. The countryside was mainly volcanic ash, and as we drove through the little towns the buildings were white-washed with green shutters and had volcanic gardens with an abundance of cactus plants.

We drove to Montana de Fuego (Fire Mountain) and rode camels to the summit along a ridge with a steep drop on either side. It was a bumpy ride, being tossed around with every step, and a little unnerving when they turned their head 180 degrees to look at you without looking where they were going. They were muzzled, which we were told prevented them from spitting on us. At the summit, we toasted our sandwiches over an opening down to the core of the volcano where temperatures reach 750 degrees Fahrenheit (400 Centigrade). We threw in pieces of wood that would burst into flames, and when we threw water in, it gushed up like a geyser.

Our next stop was La Cueva de los Verdes, a spectacular system of underground grottoes that extend for six kilometers and happen to be the longest volcanic galleries in the world. There is a concert hall in the lower cave.

Camels up to Montana de Fuego, Lanzarote of the Canary Islands

Jennifer with her friend Alice

Bimbimbi and *Melissa II* cleared the harbour early afternoon, heading for Santa Cruz de Tenerife, 146 miles away. It was wonderful sailing the whole way. Before rounding the point between Lanzarote and Fuerteventura, we were hard on the wind but then we were on a broad reach and even got the spinnaker up. When the winds were light, we pulled away from *Bimbimbi*. When winds increased and we had to reef the main, *Bimbimbi* would speed ahead . . . except at night when we had visual contact with her most of way. We arrived at our destination at the same time – around 1600 hours – having averaged 5.6 knots for the trip. Nearing the harbour, I calculated that we crossed the position of Nelson's approach for the Battle of Santa Cruz de Tenerife when he got his arm shot off. The British were defeated in that battle in 1797.

On our arrival, the first thing we had to do was chase down the module for the refrigerator. We phoned Adler-Barbour to discover it had been shipped February 16, even though it was ordered January 24. It didn't arrive until February 24, and what had been a price of $140 turned out to be $400. It brought back memories of our experience waiting for the exhaust valves in Georgetown.

That aside, we had picked the perfect time to arrive in Santa Cruz. It was the Carnival of Santa Cruz de Tenerife! Second only to the one in Brazil, it attracts people from around the world. Campers pitch their tents on whatever green space they can find in parks, in front of buildings . . . virtually anywhere there is grass. Festivities begin with a parade early Friday evening and continue all night long with people in fancy dresses, dancing into the early hours. This continues non-stop until the following Wednesday, which is Ash Wednesday. It ends with the "entierro de la sardina" (burial of the sardine) but starts up again the following weekend, known as the weekend of the *piñata*. Decorative papier mâché containers, filled with toys and candy, are smashed open with a stick, while children scurry about picking up the fallen treasures.

The beaches were beautiful, and we all went swimming for the first time since the Azores. The girls had met some school kids who had become great companions, even though they couldn't speak English and our girls didn't speak Spanish. I did repairs to the head and the forward hatch and resealed the windows, as we anxiously waited for the refrigerator part to arrive. Pat was provisioning for a month at sea, while Jennifer's job was to Vaseline the eggs to ensure their freshness.

There was still lots of activity downtown with the Carnival. The costumes, face masks, and fireworks were spectacular. We took a day off from chores and rented a car to explore more of Tenerife. The girls were more interested in hanging out with their new friends, so we tagged along with the *Bimbimbi* crew. Despite unpleasant weather the countryside was lush and we drove along a mountain ridge to La Laguna, toured the Cathedral of San Cristóbal de La Laguna, then on to Puerto de la Cruz to the Jardin Botanico (Botanical Gardens). A rubber tree there had a fascinating root system, and according to the sign, was several hundred years old.

Our next adventure was to take the cable car up Mount Teide, then walking to the top of the volcano (3770 metres), which was covered in sulfur deposits, giving it a very strong sulfur smell. The wind was strong, yet nothing we hadn't dealt with before. But for some unknown reason, each of us suffered with earache, which might have been due to the elevation.

We could have easily spent a few days touring the island, but getting ready for our Atlantic crossing was on my mind. We fueled up and topped up our water. The fridge part that was essential to have operating for the tropics didn't arrive until late afternoon on our planned departure day. Pat was still ensuring that we had enough provisions, and the girls . . . well, they just didn't want to leave. They wanted Santa Cruz to be their new home.

We had decided to make Tobago our landfall; *Bimbimbi* agreed with us. Barbados is often chosen because it is closer, but we had heard that the Port of Entry, Bridgetown's Bay, was an open roadstead and not a comfortable anchorage. We bid *Bimbimbi* farewell long before we were ready to leave. In fact, it was 1730 hours before we finally departed, about three and a half hours after her.

The first night was with rough seas and winds of force 7 and 8. By first light, it had subsided enough that we could drop the storm sail and trysail and carry a reefed main and lapper on a reach. It was exhausting crawling around the deck in the dark putting up and bagging sails. Pat and I were quite busy that first night, so we let the girls off for their watches, just until things settled down by late morning and then they did watches all day.

Having spoken to Jamie by ham radio, he informed me that he had made contact with Ashley on *Scallywag*, who having worked in Portugal with his wife, was now sailing back to Australia.

Rough conditions continued for most of the next day. Poor Jennifer was really suffering from sea sickness. We were in the trade winds, which are from the east, so we were running. On a run, the motion is severe rocking. On a beat or a reach, you may be smashing into seas, but the wind heels the boat which gives it a steadying motion. On our previous crossing, Jennifer had a much easier time than she was having now. She wasn't keeping anything down. We fed her juices until we were able to convince her to eat canned tomatoes. Things improved for her gradually, but she was suffering much more than we were. I was usually next in line for motion sickness. Pat was after me, then Julie who was seldom bothered. It took us a couple of days to get comfortable with the seas. To make matters worse, the wind activated self-steering, Ned, was of little value on a run. When we were in England, I had picked up a new Autohelm 5000 self-steering, which we had nicknamed *Dudley*. I hadn't used it much and was having trouble adjusting it for the wind conditions. The fear was of jibbing. It took a day or two for us to adjust things to work. What helped was we didn't use the main but ran a jib sheet through the end of the main boom. Then we had another jib on the other side poled out with the spinnaker pole. We sailed wing on wing, and it worked great! From that time on, we didn't use the main for the entire crossing. We still had many daily sail changes, ranging from storm sail to Spinnaker, but by the end of day two, we had things sorted out so that our self-steering was working and there was less fear of jibing.

Julie and Jennifer were back to doing night watches on our old system: Julie with me for four hours then Jennifer with Pat for the next four. The rule was there must be two on deck for sail changes. Having said that, one night I came out after my nap and the spinnaker was flying. Pat had set it by herself. At the end of our watches, we would report on traffic that was seen and anything else of interest. One night it was commercial fishing boats, which didn't respond to our radio messages. Another day we saw three British warships heading south. As it was March 1, 1982, we guessed they were heading for the Falkland Islands, due to the Argentinean invasion to claim the islands from the British.

It was incredible the amount of sail changes that went on. *Melissa II* was a tender boat as opposed to a heavy weather boat. Consequently, when winds increased, it meant a sail change. Likewise, when the winds dropped off, we would hank on larger sails. It was often brought up by our fellow boaters that we seemed to want to race all the time. Well yes, we wanted to reduce sea time whenever possible, however, when two or more boats come out of a harbour, heading for the same destination, it inevitably ends up in a race.

My radio contacts were a saving grace. It made us feel we weren't alone. There wasn't much privacy when I was on the radio because many hams enjoyed hearing seafarers' adventures. The benefit was that someone would patch in a phone call for us. A curious listener from Montreal patched in a call to my sister Joan who lived there.

Taking sextant sights for calculating our position was difficult because of the wave height. You have to see the horizon in order to observe the degrees above the horizon of the stars, moon or sun. I had to stand on top of the life raft with my arm around the mast to take a shot. Latitude is always easy to calculate accurately by noon sun shots; longitude was a bit more challenging. The sight reduction tables we were using were ones popularly used by aircraft during World War II. What would take a navigator a few minutes from an airplane to calculate took me over an hour on the boat. I tracked our position on the chart and recorded the daily mileage. We were about fifteen miles behind *Bimbimbi* most of the time, so of course, we never saw her. *Scallywag* was south of us and would make its landfall a week or so before us. She would cross our course because she was heading for Barbados, which is far north of Tobago, our landfall. It was likely we would all meet up in the Panama Canal at some later date.

We caught fish anytime we wanted, which made up most of our diet. It was mostly dorado, but we caught the occasional striped tuna as well. As our freezer filled, we would only string out a line in the afternoon to fish, using a heavy nylon line attached to a cleat on the stern. Often we would use the winch to reel in larger fish, as our speed of 6 knots made it very difficult to haul in by hand. Quite often in the morning we would find flying fish in the cockpit, but we never ate them. Some people do, but we found them very smelly. Occasionally on my night watch, one would hit me in the face while I was scanning the horizon.

We had to repair sails as clues would come adrift, chafing occurred and often rips because of the constant strain. I spent an entire day sewing our 150% genoa. We noticed that our jib halyard was badly chafed near the mast head. Fortunately, we had plenty of line and could replace it before it snapped. Pat spent a lot of the day making a courtesy flag for Tobago. We had radio contact with Rudy in Flushing, England, who gave us the news that a yacht had been stolen from St. Lucia of the Lesser Antilles. We never heard if it was recovered.

During one of Pat's night watches, she heard water rushing in and discovered that our bilge was full of water, creating instant panic. Along with our electric bilge pump, we had hooked up one operated by a foot pump. The hose had come off it, and water was pouring in. After making the repairs, we used buckets to speed up the bailing process. Everything seemed to take so much longer because of the constant pitching and rolling. Poor Jamie was having his share of problems as well. He was steering by hand because his generator that powered his self-steering was non-functional and he couldn't repair it. Thank goodness ours could be driven by the batteries. Also his steering cable broke, and he spent four hours repairing it in the middle of the night.

During my conversations with both Ashley and Jamie, I expounded on the virtues of the Virgin Islands, trying to convince them to go there. Jamie would only be about 800 miles away when in Tobago. Ashley, on the other hand, was only 600 miles, and it would be a shame to get back to Australia having missed the shining star of the Caribbean. Jamie was adamant that he wanted to get home and intended to go from Tobago to the Panama Canal. Ashley was wavering. It was brought up each time we made radio contact.

During my next contact with Rudy, he informed me that an Atlantic-wide search was on for Steve Callahan on *Napoleon Solo*, a twenty-two-foot boat that was long overdue sailing from the Canary Islands to Antigua. His family was frantically calling the Canary Islands daily to get news, which was very sad. He would have been experiencing the same sea conditions we were. Later we heard that he had been rescued after spending seventy-six days at sea in a life raft. He subsequently wrote the book, *Adrift*, which became a best-seller. Then we heard news that a German boat with man, wife and a crewmember they had picked up in Africa were headed for Barbados, but only two of them arrived. They were arrested, but I never did hear the rest of the story.

Our bright spot of the day occurred when we made radio contact with an operator from St. Catharines, Ontario. He was able to patch us by phone to Craig and Joyce Gillespie, our farmer friends from nearby Vineland. We had a wonderful, long conversation, updating them on our travels and hearing all their news.

About two thirds of the way, we saw a supertanker off in the distance. He was going very slowly. I contacted him by radio and chatted for some time. He couldn't see me at that stage, yet picked me up on his radar. *Chevron Southamerica*, overall length 1,300 feet, beam 225 feet, draught 80 feet, headed for Barbados with 480 thousand tons of oil. He gave us our position that was out by 250 miles. We were seldom out more than twenty miles even after a couple of days without sights. The captain had obviously misinterpreted the information he received from his navigator. We were on a collision course, which you can ascertain by your compass sighting if it remains unchanged. I joked by suggesting he would not have to change course as I would alter mine to pass astern. We were still an hour away from him. He cautioned me not to get to close as I would experience wind turbulence, and he was right. I was surprised at the effect when we passed his stern even though he was only going 6 knots.

He explained that his slow speed was to reduce storage costs because it was cheaper to store oil out on the ocean than at port.

Crossing the Atlantic, wing on wing

We heard from Ashley that he expected to make landfall the next day in Barbados. *Lucky him!* We still had about a third of our journey to go. Also he informed us that he was going to visit the Virgin Islands. I was very envious. If we went, it would put us into the tropical storm season going north in the Pacific. We appeared to be gaining on Jamie as we had a few days of light air that didn't slow us down but would have had a big effect on *Bimbimbi*.

We had worked our way into a comfortable routine. There were lots of sail changes that kept me busy. Pat baked bread and prepared scrumptious dinners of fish, Julie looked after our lunches, and Jennifer made date squares, cookies, or a cake, on occasion. Our four hours on and four hours off worked well. If I was really exhausted from making boat repairs and sail changes, Julie would look after most of my shift so I could rest. Jennifer did the same for Pat.

We planned our landfall at Scarborough, the capital of Tobago, only about 140 miles away. Just after midnight on March 17, Pat spotted what looked like a platform, well lit with floodlights. It must have been an offshore drilling rig. We were a long ways off, but it was still visible when Julie and I took over our shift in the early morning. I took sights during the day and discovered we had been set south-west by the Equatorial current that we had been counting on. It meant we should jibe and put up the main, which hadn't been up for nineteen days. Just as we were scurrying around taking down one jib, setting the main, taking down the spinnaker pole and moving the other jib, we caught a forty-four-inch dorado. Everything was happening at once. *Land ho!* At 1340 hours on March 17, we sighted land. At 1700 hours we entered the harbour and were greeted by *Bimbimbi*, who had arrived just a few hours earlier. Even though we were so close for the entire passage, we never caught sight of her.

From the Canary Islands to Tobago we had covered the 2,655 nautical miles in twenty days plus an hour and a half, at an average speed of 5.7 knots per hour. Our day's run ranged from 121 to 155 miles. From our starting point at Gibraltar, it was 3,607 nautical miles, with a stop in Casablanca and the Canary Islands.

The first night after a landfall was always special. The risk was over, and we didn't have to deal with watches. We were at anchor with our quarantine flag up, as we hadn't cleared customs. I celebrated by shaving off my twenty-day-old beard. *Bimbimbi* was tied up at the dock, so we took the freshly caught dorado over for dinner. The next morning, we went through the ritual of clearing customs. The police took our rifle and would return it to us upon our departure. All the authorities were very friendly and welcoming. To add to the celebrations, Jamie's mother and sister Peta had flown to Scarborough from Australia. We all went to a "Jump-Up" at the local pub with a great steel band, and we danced and danced, which was a good way regain our balance after three weeks at sea.

The real surprise was that *Scallywag* was there too. She had sailed from Barbados to Tobago to surprise us. We were delighted to meet the crew, having only got to know them through radio contact for the last month. To add to our delight, Ashley said they would also go to the Virgin Islands if I agreed to be their tour guide. The proposal was pretty hard to resist, even though we were going to expose ourselves to questionable weather in the Pacific. Once we transversed the Panama Canal, it would be summer and not a good time.

Trinidad and Tobago have undergone a lot of political changes. According to Wikipedia, Dutch, English, Spanish, Swedish, and French transformed Tobago into a battle zone, and the island changed hands thirty-three times, the most in Caribbean history. It was finally ceded to the British in 1814 under the Treaty of Paris. We had heard negative reports about Trinidad or, more specifically, Port of Spain, a major port. En route, we heard that a man and wife who had anchored in the harbour had been attacked, resulting in the woman being raped and the man murdered. It wasn't caused by Trinidadians but by crew members off a freighter in the harbour. A lot of crime was caused by crew members of visiting freighters.

We moved the three boats over to Store Bay, which was only twelve miles away. We went over to Bucco Reef in the dinghy to snorkel. When we returned, we learned that Peta had suffered a severe reaction to seasick pills and had to be taken to hospital by ambulance. The doctor prescribed Cogentin, which gave her instant relief.

For the next few days, we all had a wonderful time. On March 22, we celebrated Pat's birthday aboard *Bimbimbi*, whose upper decks were perfect to accommodate a party of twelve. Julie learned how to sailboard with Ashley's sailboard. We socialized with people who came down to our boats, just out of curiosity.

Our time in Tobago had been exciting. *We were back in the Caribbean!* Now, our life was snorkeling, swimming, sail boarding, partying, and gorging on gourmet meals. Julie was the sandwich maker for lunches; Jennifer baked cakes and squares for our desserts, while the rest of us took turns with dinners. We had met wonderful people, danced to steel bands, etc., but it was time to move on. The best part was that we would be moving on with a gang of friends to the best part of the Caribbean.

Late afternoon, we departed for Union Island, sailing through the night in favourable winds and giving Granada a wide berth because it was experiencing political unrest. In 1979, a coup established Maurice Bishop as Prime Minister of a Marxist-Leninist government. When sailing the Lesser Antilles in 1980, we heard stories of sailboats being fired upon close to harbour. It eventually ended when US Forces invaded Granada and order was restored. As we entered the Union Island harbour, we caught a Spanish mackerel, which we barbequed for dinner that night on the beach with the *Scallywag* crew. The *Bimbimbi* crew had chosen to dine at a local restaurant. When they returned to the boat, they discovered they had been broken into and money was stolen.

Things on Union Island didn't improve. We had noticed the sailboat *Hurricane* anchored in the harbour. It didn't have its home port printed on its stern, nor did it exhibit an ensign or a courtesy flag; only a Greek flag at the spreaders, which didn't make a whole lot of sense. It was used as a charter boat for taking tourists out for day cruises. The first morning, it weighed anchor, proceeding across our bow hitting our anchor chain and barely missing us. The following morning, it smashed into *Scallywag*, causing extensive damage. It didn't even stop. We reported it to the police. It appeared that the skipper was a friend of the constable, so he wasn't that concerned and suggested we sort it out ourselves. Eventually, Ashley agreed to settle out of court, accepting $200, four cases of beer and three cases of wine. You can understand why we were not all that impressed with Union Island.

After visiting Palm Island, we anchored at Sandy Cay, a short distance away, and lounged on the beach. Pat and I gave each other a haircut, a fairly common occurrence every few weeks, then dove for fish, hoping for lobster. No lobster, but we found lots of conch. Pat brushed up against a sea urchin, getting numerous spines in her ankle and that proved to be a painful experience for her.

Later we all went for dinner on Bimbimbi: conch fritters, Katrina's rice with sauce, Robin's salad, and Julie's marshmallow brownies. Out came my banjo, and we had a singsong. It was a fun evening, but to make our Union Bay experience even worse, Jamie's dinghy disappeared. We got a call on the VHF radio reporting that it had been found, but a reward was required for its return. It was obvious that it was the person who stole it. Pat's ankle got worse, with lots of swelling. She put hot candle wax on it and slept on the side berth with her leg elevated, which seemed to help.

Next stop was at Mayreau Island at Saline Bay, where we went to dive the wreck of the *Puruni*, a World War I minesweeper that sank in 1918. Afterwards, we pushed on to the island of Canouan, just over three miles long. It is an independent state within the British Commonwealth only twenty-five miles from St. Vincent. We anchored overnight before continuing on to Mustique, a small private exclusive island owned by the homeowners numbering about forty-two. At that time, you could only get there by private plane or boat. Each lot is about one hundred acres. Princess Margaret and Mick Jagger of the Rolling Stones had places there. We were told that they would attend the Jump-Up at Basel's Bar on occasion and join in with the locals for dancing.

Ray and Mike aboard *Merry Dance* from Vancouver were anchored in the harbour. They had shipped their boat to Kingston, Ontario, and had sailed along the coast to Beaufort where they went offshore to the Virgin Islands. They had met Ed and Nancy aboard *Nordlys*, as well as the *Docent* crew. They told us some horror stories about St. Lucia, which was on our route. Boaters were experiencing robberies and being threatened. In the afternoon, Jennifer, Ashley, Pat, and I took the dinghy over to view the wreck of the *Antilles*, a French cruise ship that in 1971 had wanted to treat the passengers to a view of "The beautiful island of Mustique." They hit the rocks and sank. (Sounds a little familiar, doesn't it when recalling the Costa Concordia?) The ship looked like it hadn't been touched since it sank. Lifeboats and anchors were still visible on deck. It gave off eerie sounds from inside caused by the wave motion.

Basil's Bar on the Island of Mustique

Each morning we would meet at Basil's Bar to decide on the day's activities; one day it was a walk around the Island. We visited the exclusive Cotton House Hotel where we had lunch and lounged on the balcony absorbing the gorgeous views. Back at *Melissa II*, a sailboarder came over to chat. David Grierson invited us for drinks at his home and arranged to pick us up at 1830 hours. His home was beautiful. Sliding glass walls separated the living area and indoor pool from the balcony. Ocean views were 270 degrees. He and his wife Glenna were wonderful hosts. After cocktails, it was off to Basil's Bar for the steel band and the Jump-Up.

Next morning, they joined us for coffee aboard *Melissa II*; then we departed before noon to take pictures of the *Antilles* wreck, carrying on to Petite Nevis, a small uninhabited island for a picnic lunch on the beach. The island is used for butchering whales. We photographed two whales that had recently been butchered. There was still oil on the bones, and Julie found baleen on the beach. She jumped up on the skeleton to have her picture taken. Ashley shimmied up a coconut tree to retrieve a couple of coconuts, which we enjoyed with our lunch. With the whole beach to ourselves it really was paradise!

Julie on a whale bone

In late afternoon, we left for Bequia, a small island only a few miles away. After anchoring in the harbour at Port Elizabeth and having cocktails, we went ashore for a Jump-Up with a great steel band. In the morning, we all met on *Scallywag* to discuss what Islands we would visit on our way to the Virgin Islands. Pat and I were appointed tour guides, as we had done the trip before. It was only a few miles to Kingstown on St. Vincent, our next anchorage.

We busied ourselves during the day getting supplies and filling our eighty-gallon water tank, laboriously transporting jerry cans that we filled with a hand pump then ferried them out by dinghy. It took a few hours for that chore. We congregated on *Scallywag* again that evening for a bon voyage dinner for *Bimbimbi*; she was departing in the morning on her own to head for the Virgin Islands. There was a chance that we would see her there before she left for the Panama Canal.

At 0700 the next morning, we woke up to a bit of a scare. A local was perched on the stern rail. He had swum to the boat and boarded the stern from the self-steering bracket. Pat yelled at him to get off in no uncertain terms, which he did and swam nonchalantly to shore. The scary part was that we didn't hear him boarding.

After breakfast, we departed for Martinique. At 1600 hours, we were abeam of the Pitons, two volcanic plugs on St. Lucia that can be seen from miles away. The largest peak, Soufrière, almost half a mile high, is still active and last erupted in 1979. Having heard reports from boaters that it was unsafe to leave your boat

unattended in St. Lucia because of thieves, we were denied the privilege of visiting the World Heritage Park, home of the Pitons.

The Pitons, St Lucia

Strong winds were hard on the nose but manageable. Beating like that puts a
lot of strain on the gear, and we experienced it when we heard a loud 'crack'. The
headboard tore off the jib. We often refer to winds like this as "gear busters", but
we made rapid progress and fetched the Fort-de-France harbour of Martinique at
0100 hours. It wasn't easy negotiating the entrance in the dark. Once anchored,
we all went to bed.

After clearing customs in the morning, we had to re-anchor because the
vessel *Horizon* from Nassau left the dock and, in doing so, fouled the anchor of a
nearby French vessel.

The next day, after the girls' morning shopping trip in town, we motored
across the bay for lunch and spent the rest of the day windsurfing, swimming,
and enjoying a day on the beach.

At 1800 hours, we finally set sail for Îles des Saintes, a pleasant sail in moderate winds. We bypassed Dominique, not wanting to expose the *Scallywag* crew
to the treatment we had experienced on our previous visit. We arrived at Îles
des Saintes 0930 hours. *Scallywag* arrived shortly after. For us it was revisiting
the island that we so enjoyed two years earlier. In fact, when we went ashore
to clear customs, we saw the same two girls at a table selling pastries that we

had seen two years before. They had been about twelve years old then. I don't think we had changed as much as they had in the two years. We went to the hotel for lunch, enjoying stuffed crab, fish with almonds and a banana sundae for desert.. We walked the short distance to the other side of the island and did some bodysurfing, then back to *Melissa II* for an evening of cocktails, cheese and crackers and popcorn.

Because we were enjoying the island so much, we decided to stay an extra day. Eventually we moved the boats over to a rocky rolly anchorage on the other side of the island for more windsurfing, bodysurfing, swimming and later we enjoyed a bonfire on the beach.

The next morning, we had a radio call from *Bimbimbi*. *What a surprise!* They were in the main harbour, a ten-minute walk across the island. We all weighed anchor and sailed around to join them for lunch, then for me it was a grueling day of scrubbing the boat bottom. I always thought of "Barry the Barracuda" when doing the bottom and wondered if he would remember me when we got back to Christmas Cove.

We departed for Antigua at 1800 hours to sail through the night. It was a fast but bumpy sail, with the wind hard on the nose. A wave came into the cockpit and another crashed into the hanging locker porthole, soaking everything in it. *Oh well, life at sea can be a challenge sometimes.* We fetched the harbour at 0800 hours, wet, but all was well. Our quarantine flag alerted customs, who came out immediately to clear us. Jennifer was delighted to see that *Stampeder* was there, and she had a great reunion with the kids. We all went to the barge in Falmouth Harbour for Happy Hour, where rum and coke was a dollar, then on to *Scallywag* for dinner.

Saint Barthélemy, or St. Barts, is one of four territories that make up the French West Indies, the others being St. Maarten, Guadeloupe, and Martinique. Beginning in the early 1600s, it was French, then taken over by Britain who gave it to the Swedes, who in 1887 gave it back to the French. Today it has a reputation as being a tourist spot for the rich and famous.

We hadn't been to St. Barts on our Caribbean excursion two years earlier because it was south and quite a bit east of St. Maarten and north and quite a bit east of Antigua. It means beating into the trade winds. This time with more favourable winds, it was a comfortable sail with wind on the quarter. We fetched Gustavia, capital of St. Barts, at 0830 hours. Clearing customs would have cost us for overtime because it was Sunday and they were closed. We spent the entire day visiting fellow yachters, recognizing many and meeting new ones. Julie and Jennifer were in the habit of inflating the dinghy and checking out the yachts in the harbour. We were accustomed to seeing them holding onto the gunnels, gabbing with the owners in the cockpit. This would encourage a wave to us and a motion to come over, resulting in meeting many interesting friends.

The next morning, we cleared customs and went into town for groceries but spent most of the day tending ship's chores, including sending Pat up the mast in the boson's chair to retrieve a halyard. We finally departed with *Scallywag* at 1600 hours in a perfect following wind for our spinnaker but had to steer by hand because it was a bit of a reach and the spinnaker is very sensitive to slight course changes. We sailed on through the night, opening up a substantial lead on *Scallywag*. Spotting land in early morning, we hove to waiting for *Scallywag* to catch up, then rounded the tip of St. John, guiding them into Cruz Bay, US Virgin Islands, making our landfall at 1400 hours. This was exciting! We were home again!

We cleared customs and got a cruising permit. After spending time with friends it was back to chores. I repaired the alternator, took some sails in for repair, went to the bank for money, picked up groceries, and then ran into Andy, skipper aboard *Wind River*, a Hinckley 64. We went back to his boat for a catch-up. People were surprised to see us as they didn't expect us to come back to the Virgin Islands. Everyone we ran into was curious about where we had been for the last two years, which naturally led to lots of socializing. It was amazing how we kept running into the same people on both sides of the Atlantic.

We walked to Cruse Bay to enjoy the quaint shops and lunch at the restaurant then back to the boats to swim. I had an interesting experience! I dove off the boat and was joined immediately by a large porpoise, about my size. I was very uncomfortable and got out of the water. When I think of it now, I wish I had stayed in and made contact with it.

That evening we went to the Rosewood Resort to listen to the steel band on the patio. In the morning, *Bimbimbi* arrived. Julie and Jennifer picked them up in our dinghy and took them into customs, then we all got together on *Melissa II* to do some spinnaker flying. Even though we were the smallest boat, we had the largest spinnaker. We would anchor from the stern then hoist the spinnaker with the boson's chair tied to the sheets (lines) on each corner, then get in the chair and trim the sheets to fill the spinnaker, letting out lots of halyard to get it far away from the boat. We all had a go. Julie got the highest and was straight out about forty feet off the water. *What a thrill!*

Spinnaker Flying

We took the dinghy to Cruse Bay and dined at the Lobster Pot, listening to live music and socializing with other patrons. The next morning, we left for Christmas Cove, our favourite snorkeling spot. I didn't have to scrub the bottom, so I didn't get to see if "Barry the Barracuda" was still there and whether he would remember me. After snorkeling, we continued on to Charlotte Amalie. The girls visited friends in town and went back to *Scorpio* for dinner. Pat and I went to a dinner presentation for timeshares at Megan's Bay. Located on the North Atlantic side with a beautiful white sandy beach. it was once owned by Arthur Fairchild, who gave most of it as a gift to the Municipality of St. Thomas and St. John in 1943 for use as a public park. Smitten by the presentation, we bought a timeshare with a down payment and agreed to monthly payments. About a year later, we got a letter from our salesman, informing us that he had been fired and the whole operation was going bankrupt. Thank goodness he let us know or we would have continued with the payments.

Carnival was on in Charlotte Amalie! It was quite an affair but not quite as grandiose as the one in Santa Cruz, Tenerife, Canary Islands. Pat and I went over to *Scorpio* for a dinner, while the girls went to town with friends to take part in the festivities. As we could see them from the boat, we didn't bother going in. Mike went in town but probably wished he hadn't. It was late when he started back to *Scallywag,* and taking a shortcut through an alleyway, he was attacked by three men, who knocked him to the ground and stole his wallet. It was hardly worth reporting, as the police were overworked that night. In the morning, I took the dinghy to pick up Sally; however, I wasn't greeted with much enthusiasm. When Mike got home after his robbery, they began to party and it carried on all night.

Back on *Melissa II,* we departed on our tour of the British Virgin Islands. Pat, Sally, and I did the tourist thing in town. Pat was suffering with back pain, and we just happened to run into Dr. Osborne. He prescribed something I couldn't pronounce and advised her to call him Monday if it didn't improve. I called the Last Resort to make reservations for that evening.

The girls overslept the following morning, so I got up and made pancakes to get things started. Pat's back was a lot better, so after breakfast, we left for the Baths only ten miles away. We dove the caves, which was always such an amazing experience. We didn't leave until 1700 hours for Trellis Bay on Beef Island, a stone's throw from Tortola. It is a favourite anchorage for Canadians, usually including quite a contingent from Ottawa.

Next morning, Pat and I went over to visit on *Jolly Dan* to get caught up on the Ottawa news. Since Pat and I grew up there, we knew many of the Ottawa crowd that annually anchored in Trellis Bay. Then we enjoyed a nice sail to Deadman's Bay on Peter Island. Pat and I spent most of the day doing boat and sail repairs, including fixing the jammed bow roller, before going to shore and making our way over to the coconut grove on the south side of the island. We gathered about a dozen coconuts, part of our food supply for our passage to the Panama Canal. *Lucky me!* The girls all participated in preparing a sumptuous dinner, including Jennifer's apple cake, then it wasn't long before we were ready for bed.

We sailed over to Roadtown for Pat's appointment with Dr. Osborne. Julie and Sally went ashore to do some shopping, while Jennifer stayed on board at Village Cay Marina to continue with her school work. After clearing customs, we sailed to Red Hook on St. Thomas, cleared US customs, fueled up and filled the water tanks in preparation for our departure to the Panama Canal. From there we sailed to Christmas Cove. The only boat anchored there, *Mathew*, happened to belong to our friends Pat and Don, whom we hadn't seen for two years, so it was nice to see them again.

It was raining next morning when we left for Charlotte Amalie. With little wind, we motored with Julie at the helm. She brought us up close to *Bimbimbi* and *Scallywag*.

We all went out for dinner that evening and said goodbye to our dear friends. It was the last night that we were all together so it was kind of sad. We said goodbye to the *Bimbimbi* crew, who had acquired a crew member, Tim, but he decided to go with *Scallywag* instead. They were going to be leaving the next morning on their own. It was sad because we had been sailing with them for four months. We might see her at the Panama Canal, but weren't certain.

In the morning, *Scallywag* joined us to sail over to Lindbergh Bay. We all walked Sally to the airport for her departure. We were going to miss her. She was flying to San Francisco to visit with relatives, and it was quite possible we would see her there. I scrubbed the bottom, deflated the dinghy, and fastened it tightly on the life raft, then after clearing customs, we were off. It was 1700 hours on April 29.

CHAPTER 13
To the Panama Canal

"Hark, now hear the sailors cry, smell the sea, and feel the sky let your soul and spirit fly."

– Van Morrison

After hearing stories of piracy off the coast of Columbia, we devised a code system with *Scallywag* to give each other our position over the radio. Also, we intended to stay off the coast at least eighty miles to avoid Columbian fishing boats which might have posed a threat. Winds were light, which was a bit of a surprise. We had a close encounter with a tug towing a barge, which didn't have any lights on and we almost crossed over the tow line.

By 0600 hours the next morning, we started to motor and continued all day. It was not an ocean passage we were used to or expecting. It was very comfortable. Jennifer baked cookies and did school work, and Julie helped in the cockpit and also did school work. They were not expecting to be able to continue their studies while on this passage, so this worked out well. The sooner they could send in their last and final school assignment, the better. They were a bit apprehensive about going into the school system in the fall once we reached Victoria. After all, it had been three years since they had attended school.

While motoring, we could get close to *Scallywag*, close enough to pass them some of Jennifer's cookies. We had motored thirty-six hours and used up six gallons of diesel fuel before the wind came up and we could sail. Granted, we sometimes were helped along with a little wind. The four of us sat in the cockpit talking about what we would do when we made our landfall in Victoria. Pat and I would be looking for a job, while we continued to live on the boat at a marina until Christmas.

By late afternoon, the wind came up on our beam, and I was able to put up the spinnaker. I took sextant sights and had fixed our position on the chart. We were actually a few miles ahead of our dead reckoning as a result of a slight favourable current. To make things even better, I caught a forty-inch wahoo, which I gutted and cut into steaks for dinner and had plenty left over to freeze. I had a QSO with Bill in Florida. It was great to be back in contact with him, the first time since the previous summer. He was able to find someone in Tucson to patch in a phone call to my mother in Tucson. She was anxious to know when we were going to be in San Francisco, as she intended to meet us there.

Night watches were enjoyable; Julie and I would sit in the cockpit and talk about Victoria. Pat and Jennifer did the same thing when it was their turn. Normally, on watch, we would stay down below, coming up every ten minutes or so to scan the horizon for traffic. There was more urgency to stay in the cockpit now because we were in a questionable area for safety. Pat was still suffering with back pain so I insisted that she wake me up to do any sail changes during her watch.

We were on day five now and, for the first time, we had strong winds and rough seas. We sailed with the lapper and reefed main. Things got a little hot and humid inside, but I couldn't open the hatches to let air in because water was coming over the deck. We got cooled off in the cockpit throwing buckets of water over each other. Later in the day, we were able to hank on the 180 genoa then the spinnaker. With all the hatches and windows open, it was a lot more pleasant. We lost sight of *Scallywag* but kept radio contact; using our code system for our long lat. which we devised to hide our location from potential pirating. Off the coast of Columbia, it is a big concern. When I made contact with Bill on the ham radio again in the evening, he patched a phone call to my sister Joan in Montreal. She was anxious to know where we were. I responded that we were enjoying the Caribbean, however, changed the subject, as you just never knew who might be listening. Bill also tried someone in San Francisco to reach Sally, but no luck. We caught a nice size tuna, but before I could get it in, a shark ate it and took my hook as well.

We saw three vessels coming from the Panama Canal and talked to an Italian freighter coming from Vancouver. *Scallywag* caught up to us; they passed us some magazines, and we gave them cake that Jennifer had made. We discussed where we would make our landfall and agreed on Provenir, San Blas Islands, because there we could clear customs. It was only a few miles away and a much easier passage than expected. We had covered 960 miles in 7 days, 15.5 hours, averaging 5.25 knots.

What a paradise! The white sandy beaches and lovely palm trees were like something in *National Geographic*. Within moments, women in dugout canoes converged on us, selling molas, which use a reverse appliqué technique to form part of the traditional costume of Kuna Indian women. We bought two for $20. Pat jumped in the water and swam over to chat with Tim and Mike, while Ashley, Julie, and I swam over to greet *Samantha* from California.

After clearing, we carried on to Chimchimos Cays to lay over for a few days. The next morning we sailed to Holandes Cays, which was only fifteen miles away. Another gorgeous island! Again, it was a small island, with about a dozen palm trees, encircled by white sandy beach. We were completely on our own. We dove and got lobster, squid, grunts, squirrel fish and conch, before a shark showed up. We alerted everyone. Mike was a little slow swimming to the dinghy, and the shark was swimming along behind him. When we yelled at him, he stopped and turned around to see it and it had stopped too. Each time Mike stopped, the shark would stop. It was very amusing to recall once we hauled Mike into the dinghy.

It was late when we finished snorkeling so rather than go ashore and build a bonfire, we went over to *Scallywag* for a wonderful feast of conch fritters, lobster and Pat's fresh beer bread, followed by Jennifer's cake. I think I heard someone say: "Living on a boat isn't that bad, is it?"

Next day after a breakfast of fried fish, we donned our snorkel gear for another day in the water. Jennifer had a wonderful time playing with the colourful little fish. She would poke them with her finger, and we could hear her laughing under water in her snorkel. She seemed to be oblivious to any danger of sharks, so I kept a strict eye on her. It was a bonus that none showed up, and we got more lobster and grunts.

Ashley's water pump was giving him problems again, so most of the morning was spent effecting repairs, but the tea and scones gave us some relief. Once it was repaired, we motored over to Carti Village, another *National Geographic* centrepiece in the San Blas Islands. This tiny island was crammed with grass shacks on dirt floors. In fact, one outhouse was on stilts overhanging the ocean.

Carti Village in the San Blas Islands

Julie fell right in with the native children

With no source of drinking water, islanders would take their canoes to the mainland, Columbia, to get jugs of water every day. The people were extremely friendly. The women were dressed in colourful molas from head to toe to protect themselves from bugs. It was extremely hot, but you had to keep well covered. A small child took Julie's hand and led her around the village. The dugout canoes were painted in bright colours, and for sails, they used cloth bags sewn together. It really makes you wonder why we have to have so much when they are so happy with so little.

We left to clear customs at Provenir, only seven miles away. We met Judy and Urgen aboard *Pergrin* from Vancouver, anchored in the harbour. After scrubbing the bottom, deflating the dinghy and securing it on the life raft, I invited everybody over to *Melissa II* for dinner. It was a fun evening. After everyone left, I had a QSO with Bill in Florida before we weighed anchor. Before dark, we headed for Cristobal in Panama. It rained all night and was sweltering, hot and buggy. Pat and I spent the night in the cockpit. There was a lot of traffic but no real problems. I got Jamie on the ham radio. He had cleared the canal and was on his way to the Galapagos.

We arrived in Cristobal just before noon and only had to wait a couple of hours to get cleared by authorities. Afterwards, we tied up at the dock and then went to town to get further clearances and pay fees for the canal. Interestingly enough, I had to pay more than Ashley. When I questioned it, they explained that because my boat was smaller, it fell into another category. It was a way of getting more money out of smaller boats. Maybe if my boat was thirty feet instead of twenty-nine, I might have paid the same as Ashley.

Because France had built the Suez Canal they felt they were best-suited to build a canal joining the Caribbean with the Pacific Ocean. First they had to decide on a canal route. Many considered Nicaragua was most appropriate, but the decision was made to pass through Columbia. After all, it was only forty-two nautical miles. In 1881, the French began construction on the Panama Canal but because of mismanagement, corruption and bankruptcy, the Americans took it over completing it in 1913, thirty-two years later. Because of disease and accidents during construction, it is estimated that 500 lives per mile were lost. When it began, ownership of the canal territory was Columbian, but it went to France and then the United States. Today it is owned by the Panamanian Government. In fact, the Republic of Panama was formed when Columbia was losing interest in the canal and made it difficult for its construction, so Panama seceded from them in 1903. In spite of this jurisdiction, the Canal Zone remained with the United States until they turned it over to the Panamanians in 1999. The riveting book, *The Path Between the Seas,* by Davis McCullough, gives an in-depth view of the canal's history.

It was uncomfortable walking around downtown Colón, the city at the entrance of the canal. With unemployment at 80%, people were pretty desperate. We walked across a field to a gas station to fill a couple of jerry cans with diesel fuel and were followed back to the Yacht Club by a couple of desperate-looking fellows. Fortunately, the Yacht Club had a chain-link fence eight feet high, so you felt safe once inside. A few days earlier we had heard that a yachter had slipped through the fence for fresh air and was attacked and had his pants stolen with his wallet in them. Another yachter had his pants ripped off in a grocery store during the day. He bit the person on the leg but lost his wallet. When we got back to *Melissa II,* Pat announced that she wasn't going to go to town again. She also denied the girls their allowance because they had been derelict in their chores of tidying up the boat. She was in a great mood. You can bet I behaved myself.

The next day I had to get some money from the bank, a floor-to-ceiling glass building, so anyone on the street could see banking activity. I was wearing shorts without pockets and a tee-shirt, so when I got cash I jammed it in my underwear, which I was used to doing. Leaving the bank, I noticed a young man trembling with excitement. He was across the street but followed me. Soon he was joined by two other guys. When they crossed over to my side, I broke into a run with them in pursuit. It was about a block to the gate entrance, and fortunately I made it to the safety of the chain-link fence well ahead of them.

The Yacht Club had a bar that was open twenty-four hours every day, which was wonderful because it was air conditioned. It was mid-May, and the temperatures were unbearable: flies were everywhere. We spent most of the day in the club to escape the heat, but also meals were very affordable. It was going to be a few days before we could begin going through the canal. We met Chris and Val from England, who were looking for a crewing position. *Windward Passage* - a gorgeous wooden maxi boat - was tied up next to us and we socialized with the captain and crew members. They invited us for lunch, and once they determined that we were going to stop in San Diego, they offered to take us racing aboard *Windward Passage* when we got there.

Jennifer found a new friend, Reiner Nussbaum aboard *Kriter Lady*, a maxi boat that his father purchased from Patriarche Wines. It was being delivered from France to the United States, and Reiner was on board. The next day many of us boarded the train for Panama City. Jennifer and Tim stayed behind. We visited the Balboa Yacht Club to get information on transiting the canal, then bused into town to El Panama Hilton. Ashley and Mike took off in another direction, but we made plans to meet at the hotel later for lunch. On their walk, a car stopped with an American driver who pointed out that they were headed into an undesirable part of town and offered to drive them through it. They accepted and were quite happy they had.

We all met at the Hilton and lined up for a Chinese Restaurant. While waiting to be seated, I noticed a newspaper with the headline, "Gilles Villeneuve fue asesinado." When I translated for Julie that Gilles had been killed in practice for the Belgium Grand Prix on May 8, 1982, she burst into tears. She was an avid follower of Formula One racing and a fan of our Canadian entrant. After lunch we walked to the market and loaded up with fresh fruit and vegetables, and then got onto a bus and headed back to the Balboa Yacht Club. There we met Don, Donna Sitez, and their sons, Mike and Mark. Don was in the armed forces living in Panama, and his son Mark had agreed to be our fifth crew member to transit the canal, the rules being that you had to have five crew members and a pilot to transit the canal.

We bused to the train station to discover that there was no train. Don's son drove us to the next train station, where there was only a freight train. Australians are great at getting what they want. Ashley convinced the conductor to take us standing on the flatbed freight car to Colón, an interesting ride through the jungle. You could hear monkeys and a variety of jungle sounds. When we arrived at the marina, Mike discovered that he was missing his wallet. Jennifer was entertaining Tim and Reiner aboard *Kriter Lady*. She hadn't missed us and had a busy day of school work, baking desserts and socializing.

We were notified that we were scheduled to transit the canal in two days. That gave us one day to stock up on groceries, do laundry, shower, stash the dinghy away, and be ready for the next morning. Mike had gone to the train station and recovered his wallet. The farewell dinner was aboard *Melissa II*. The

Scallywag crew joined us for pizza, Robin's cannelloni, and Jennifer's "Goodbye Good Luck" cake.

Our pilot, Barry, arrived at 0900 hours, and we took off for the first lock. It was May 17, 1982. Our pilot had gone through with *Windward Passage* just a few days earlier. We tied up along *Scallywag,* who in turn was rafted to a tug. Three locks took us up eighty-five feet to Gatun Lake. It was stifling hot, and there was oncoming traffic, so we could stop for a swim. We had just got in the water when a passing cruise ship radioed us that they could see alligators near us and advised us to get out of the water. *We did!* It rained for the rest of the day on our descent. Finally, we ended our long day at 1730 hours by anchoring off the pilot station on Flamenco Island. A launch came for Barry and took Mark to shore, where his dad was waiting to take him home. Tim and Mike were going to Panama City for a flight back to England. We were sad to see them go, after being together a long time and forming quite a friendship. We went over to *Scallywag* for tea and Jennifer's squares and made a schedule for radio contact, as we were going to be saying goodbye then. It was an end to an exhausting day.

It was up early morning and into the fuel dock to top up our tanks and say our goodbyes to Ashley and Robin before going north. Robin went back to Colón to crew for another yacht, while Ashley worked on the cooling system at the Balboa Yacht Club. It was very sad knowing that it was unlikely we would ever see them again. We left at 0900 hours and we were on our way to Victoria.

CHAPTER 14

Panama to Victoria

"The days pass happily with me wherever my ship sails."

– Joshua Slocum

We had light winds and spent a lot of the first day motor sailing. I made contact with Bill – K4 GSQ – in Florida and also picked up Jamie on *Bimbimbi,* who had departed the Galapagos and was heading for Australia. We also talked to Ashley who was still at the Balboa Yacht Club working on the cooling system.

There was a tremendous amount of ship traffic so we maintained a twenty-four-hour watch system in the cockpit, which is very tiring, especially at night. By 0900 hours the next day, we had covered 130 miles, rounding Peninsula de Azuero. Visibility was not that great, so we gave it a wide birth. Winds were light and it rained all day, but things brightened up for us when we caught a skip jack tuna for dinner. We were heading for Golfito, Costa Rica, but had to pass Punta Burica, a point of land shared with Panama that juts out into the Pacific. With no sun and no lights visible on Punta Burica, I had no idea of our position, so we headed south to get offshore and give the point a wide birth. When it cleared up, we headed towards the entrance, eventually getting a bearing on the light. That confirmed our location, and heading into the bay, we were treated to a spectacular display of hundreds of porpoises speeding ahead, then as if by a signal, they turned and crossed our bow, jumping and splashing at the same time. We dropped anchor at 0700 hours opposite Captain Tom's, a mochilero's (backpacker) hangout, and, exhausted, I immediately crashed out.

Golfito is the main shipping dock for Chiquita Bananas. After a couple hours sleep we inflated the dinghy and went to clear customs. The wharfinger was extremely helpful and made us feel very welcome. In fact, he gave us eighty pounds of bananas. He also warned us that stealing was a thriving business there. We had a bad experience when we bought some ice-cream, getting short-changed by $12. And while the girls had dinner on *Melissa II*, Pat and I had a wonderful Chinese dinner for $4.41, and the taxi ride home was a mere twenty-three cents.

We departed 0500 hours for Puntarenas (Spanish for "sandy point"), only 165 miles away. Throughout the day, winds were variable in direction and strength, ranging from calm to squalls. Continually changing sails was very tiring, all in sweltering heat and pouring rain. The night was black, with no moon and no stars, so we had to rely on dead reckoning. From 0330 hours on, it was really nerve-racking as squalls clobbered us, one tearing out the hank of the main-sail. Our charts were small scale, with very little coverage of the shallow inner harbour. The wind picked up making me nervous about entering, so we hove to for a couple of hours until a ferry appeared and we followed it in. It was noon before we finally dropped anchor in front of the Pacific Marina, and I collapsed from exertion and spent the rest of the day in bed. Pat rested and wrote letters, while the kids worked on finishing their year's studies to be mailed. After a few hours' sleep, I made radio contact with Bill in Miami, and he found someone close to Vineland to patch in a call to Craig and Joyce. Julie made popcorn, and we spent the rest of the evening relaxing and chatting.

The next morning, we inflated the dinghy, put the motor on, and headed into the marina office. The dinghy dock and showers were $3.00 per day. The marina staff were very friendly and a great help in sending us in the right direction. We went to the customs office, and they had to come out to our boat to complete the entrance papers. They made things as easy for us as possible and stayed for a beer and some of Julie's chocolate brownies. We were cautioned about theft and encouraged to lock our dinghy and remove the motor each evening. We found the townsfolk very friendly, helpful, and obliging.

We stayed for a week, and it rained every day. Pat, Julie, and I took the two-hour bus ride to San José the first day, while Jennifer stayed to do school assign-ments. Prices were low. The seventy-mile bus trip was eighty cents. Meals were so cheap in Puntarenas that we had dinner out every night.

Julie had finished three years of correspondence school work and mailed her last assignment in Puntarenas. We were really proud of both girls for being so dil-igent with their assignments. This is how Julie describes Correspondence School:

Our first year of correspondence, Jennifer was in fourth grade, and I was in seventh. It took us a while to get into the habit of doing our school work as there were so many fun things to do, especially in the Virgin Islands. Many times mom had to tell us to get going.

Here is some information on our subjects and how we do them: grades 4. 5 and 6 are divided into three units with thirteen lessons in each unit. You are expected to do one lesson per week. For those grades, the subjects were reading, writing, spelling language or communications, math, and social studies. Each lesson is divided into days, and you do each subject in order. They explain what you are to do with examples. Then you do the assignments to be sent in each week to the Correspondence Branch to be marked by a teacher. She makes comments and usually adds a personal note. Grade 7 and 8 are a little different. You have thirty-six lessons for each subject. The subjects were reading, writing, spelling, communications, math, geography, history, and science. They are very well explained and, after you get the hang of it, easy to do. Like the others, each lesson is mailed weekly and is marked by the teacher.

After 8th grade, you start choosing your subjects. You have to take English, math, history, geography, and science, but you usually have a choice of three or four courses for each subject you choose. They don't start languages until grade 9, though I tried to start earlier. I am taking French now, and it is very well organized. They supply you with text books, tapes, and their own books full of instructions, exercises, puzzles, and things to make learning easier. Each subject is sent separately to a teacher to mark (instead of directly to the Correspondence Branch).

All the courses are provided with text books, papers, envelopes, and instructions. After the teacher has graded your papers, they are sent to an address (to our friends) in Ontario. Our friends send them on to us where ever we happen to be. We decide when we want to work. We take a lot of vacations from school but are always able to catch up. We don't do any work on passages because it is usually too rough, and looking down at your work makes you sick to your stomach. We are able to do our work at our own speed. I often wonder if I will be behind when we get back to a regular school, as a lot of our text books are quite old. We will just have to wait and see.

(When they went back to the public school system in Victoria, British Columbia, they both went into enriched programs because they were ahead with their studies.)

Now we were ready to depart and continue our trip north. We were safe along the coast of Costa Rica, but further north was complicated by the fact that Nicaragua, El Salvador, and Guatemala were engaged in brutal civil wars. El Salvador, the worst, was consumed by the communist party in 1980, like what had occurred in Granada and Cuba, where children were recruited and provided with assault weapons. It was unsafe for yachts to be within eighty miles of the coast. We gave it 120 just to be on the safe side but this exposed us to the full force of the Japanese current flowing south. Then to make matters worse, there were reports of a tropical storm brewing. We were steering a course going northwest. By 1730 hours, we were abeam of Cabo Blanco and carried on that course to get us well offshore. We kept our ears to the radio on reports of the tropical depression named 2 E. So far only two days out of Puntarenas, we had winds of 20 knots from the north. We were able to make good time on a beat with double-reefed main and our lapper and had the comfort of knowing we could scoot back to Costa Rica if the storm developed.

It was now June 1, 1982. Winds were light still from the north, and it was clear skies. Our objective was to reach Puerto Madero, Mexico, only six days from Puntarenas. We sighted *Prince Rupert City* en route to Newport News, Virginia, from Japan. He gave us a position that confirmed our dead reckoning and my sights. No news on E 2. The big thrill today was to see dozens of huge sea turtles floating on the surface. We circled them to take pictures. I talked to the Maritime Marine network and reported my position. They informed us that winds were going to increase overnight to 35 knots directly in our path. Had it been a tropical storm, we would have hightailed it back to Costa Rica, but 35 knots we could handle. Winds did pick up but nowhere near that. It was an easy night, but constant watches from the cockpit were necessary. Four hours of sitting in the cockpit could be boring but necessary in case of traffic or heavy squalls.

Our position on the chart in the morning put us twenty-five miles from Puerto Madero. We were greeted by olive-coloured sea porpoises and then sighted land at 0900 hours. The coast was featureless so we had to rely on our dead reckoning to fetch entrance to the harbour, and we were right on. We anchored between two yachts, a maxi boat and a Canadian boat. They had left by the time we cleared customs. There was a Mexican Navy gun boat tied up at the dock, and the captain insisted we raft up to them for safety reasons. He invited us aboard for tea down below in the dining area. The heat was unbearable! Flies covered the walls like wallpaper. We had never seen so many. It was such a relief to get on shore. There was no fuel dock, and we were desperate for fuel. The Navy was a great help by arranging for a truck with two forty-five-gallon drums of diesel to come down to the boat, then they filled jerry cans and passed them down to us. We went into town to an ice cream kiosk and discovered that the clerk didn't speak Spanish or English, only Mayan.

Back on *Melissa II*, it was very uncomfortable having an armed guard watching over us, as our deck was about ten feet lower than the naval vessel's deck. It wasn't hard to sense that their main interest was the three blonds onboard, but we were grateful for their earlier help. It was a dreadful night with stifling heat and hoards of flies, and a horrible smell. It was worse than we had experienced at Colon. At least there we had an air-conditioned bar open twenty-four hours a day to give us some relief.

After a sleepless night, we departed with great pleasure at 06:30 hours. With no wind, we motored for eight hours and only averaged 4.6 knots, fighting a slight current. There were lots of fishing boats to wave at. By nightfall, we encountered thunderstorms and torrential rain for two hours. Winds were in every direction, so it was a night of constantly changing sails and coming about (changing sails in the pouring rain and getting soaked isn't so bad in the sweltering heat). As the day progressed, winds piped up and it was comfortable sailing. We caught two dorados, which I cleaned and stuffed in the freezer. A school of them followed us for hours, something we had never seen before. The dorado in the Pacific are called mahi mahi.

We were crossing the Gulf of Tehuantepec, where winds resemble the mistrals in the Mediterranean. You are advised to sail with one foot on the shore or go offshore to Hawaii because torrential winds can come up quickly. We were only a mile or two offshore. Navigating was simple, and we were enjoying a lot of dolphins forging ahead of us. We were passing little settlements with picturesque old churches with a mixture of white sandy beaches and craggy cliffs. Puerto Angel signaled the end of the Gulf of Tehuantepec. This pretty little Mexican town had grass shacks on the beach, an old fort, and many beautiful buildings that we enjoyed looking at through binoculars. Our eighty pounds of bananas were all ripe now, so anyway you could cook, mix, or eat a banana, we did. Fortunately, we had given quite a few away in Puntarenas.

We were getting very poor mileage under motor and expected it was from the fuel that was quite black. This coupled with the current against us made it tough slugging. We had decided to stop at Acapulco. We would need fuel by that time, and it would be a welcome break after eleven or twelve days at sea under these grueling conditions. We had to be on watch in the cockpit night and day. Thank goodness for self-steering. Being close to shore, we could navigate by identifying landmarks during the day, but at night, it was nerve-racking when no lights or features were seen. One day was highlighted by the appearance in the water of hundreds of snakes, like nothing we had seen before. They were only about two feet long, bright green with a yellow stripe, except for the last four or five inches of their tail that was checkered in the same colours.

We were only a couple of days away from Acapulco now. The wind piped up, and there was thunder and lightning. Knowing the speed of sound is 1,100 feet per minute, I could calculate the location of the storm by counting the seconds between a lightning flash and the thunder clap. It was advancing to the point that they coincided. Winds initially were from the north-west, then swung to the south-west. We were going from a port tack to starboard tack throughout the day and night. I spent a lot of time on deck changing sails, as wind strength varied continuously. By 05:30, we could see the lights at Acapulco. Our depth sounder read fifteen fathoms, confirming our position as twenty miles, or only about four hours, away.

What a beautiful city! Palatial homes built into the cliffs and glamorous hotels, a spectacular sight when entering the harbour. At 0900, we tied up Med style (stern to) at the Acapulco Yacht Club, very posh, for the reasonable cost of $6 per day providing us with showers, swimming pool, electricity, and very courteous service. The inspector came aboard and made quite a fuss about us not having fumigation papers. We went to town to fill out a lot more paperwork for customs, obtaining a temporary import permit and a fishing license, all at different locations. We went into some nicely laid-out department stores. There were a lot of hustlers who detracted from the city's beauty.

After returning to *Melissa II*, it was back to boat maintenance. I changed the oil and filter and installed a new throw-out bearing that, fortunately, I had. Pat didn't like it when I did engine maintenance, because the engine happened to be in our living space, and I guess I made a bit of a mess with tools on the kitchen counter. To make matters worse, she had to dive overboard to move the prop shaft back and forth for me to install the bearing.

We all went out for dinner, then back to the boat for banana cake that Julie had made as we still had plenty of bananas. I hadn't put the steps back leading from the cockpit to down below. Jennifer didn't notice and had a bad fall, landing on her head and hurting her back. We gave her some pills to help with the pain. Julie slept in the cockpit because it was much cooler.

The next morning, I cleaned the bottom, which was covered in barnacles, while Pat did a hand laundry. We took a bus into town to finish clearing customs, picked up some groceries, and took a taxi back to the Yacht Club. Moored next to us was *Scorpio*, but not the same one we had met in the Caribbean. It was a Hatteras 53 being delivered from Alabama to Newport, California, by Ron and crew members Mike and Richard. Kelly, the owner, turned out to be a great tour guide.

Pat and I went back to town to pick up a few maintenance items for the boat, and then took a stroll along the beach. Back on board *Melissa II,* in sweltering heat, we had to keep hatches and windows closed because it was raining so hard.

The next day, we were tourists. Kelly insisted on taking Pat and me for a tour in a taxi he had hired. Our first stop was the Casablanca Hotel. What gorgeous views! It focused on the inner harbour, and we could see little *Melissa II* amongst the vessels twice her size. From there we went to the El Mirador, which had views of the Pacific Ocean and a platform looking over to La Quebrada where we watched the cliff divers. They have been performing since the late 1930s, gaining worldwide attention in the early 1960s from the Elvis Presley movie, *Fun in Acapulco*. The divers leap from a cliff forty metres above the ocean, equivalent to thirteen stories! They have to time their dives for an incoming swell because the depth can be less than two metres. It is a remarkable spectacle! Divers will spend a few moments to bless themselves before choosing the appropriate time to jump when a swell provides a good depth.

That was a hard act to follow, but we carried on to the prestigious Princess Hotel. Howard Hughes resided here until his death, which is thought to have happened there or on a plane leaving from there. We went for drinks at the Grotto, where you swim from the pool, under a waterfall, then sit on a stool in the water at the bar amongst gorgeous people. Acapulco has certainly gained favour with the rich and famous. I didn't fit into either category. It has been a favourite with movie stars. Today it is not without its problems with corrupt policemen and drug trafficking.

We befriended two Mexican girls, Rebecca and Patricia, and took them for lunch at Los Rancheros then back to *Scorpio* for drinks. Julie and Jennifer joined us, and Ron took the girls for a tour of the harbour on a Boston Whaler with a 35 hp Evenrude. They had a wonderful time, and Julie raved about it. Guess my 15 hp just doesn't cut it anymore. After a swim in the pool, Mike and Ron took the girls to see the cliff divers before dinner. Pat and I organized the boat, showered, and went to bed, as we were going to depart the next morning. Although we stayed only three days, we had seen lots and had a wonderful time thanks to Kelly, our personal tour guide.

Our new friends were up and bid us farewell even though it was 0800 hours. We topped up our water tanks and were off, motoring in calm seas; however, as the day progressed, winds came up from the west and the seas were very sloppy. With the hatches and windows closed, the heat down below was unbearable. We'd need to stop for fuel but didn't have a location in mind.

The next day, June 13, was our anniversary. I presented Pat with a poem I had written for her, and she was touched:

It's only fitting that you and me
should celebrate this day upon the sea
It's great expanse seems to signify
our joys and dreams of days gone by
and endless more yet to come
that seem to surface with each days run
but best of all my dreams to come true
is that I can spend each day with you.

I couldn't offer much more than that because I was really sick and spending quite a bit of time on the throne. I went two days with nothing but Jello and water. Jennifer was also very sick with stomach cramps and vomiting. It was quite likely the result of the Mexican food we had been enjoying. We were lucky that we had a registered nurse onboard, who fed us Codeine and Ampicillin.

Abeam of Punta Cabeza Negro, I calculated our average speed was 4.3 knots, even with our clean bottom. I figured we were fighting a current of .5 to .7 knots. As a result of the thick, black Mexican diesel fuel, fuel consumption was almost double what it should have been. However, at nine cents a gallon, I guess we couldn't complain. Winds were from the west during the day, so we would be fighting a lee shore, which meant the waves had the full width of the Pacific to build up. They were hitting our port side and splashing into the cockpit.

Now, after four days, I was concerned about our fuel consumption. This coupled with weather warnings of tropical depression E 3 convinced me that we should put into shore. The storm was 400 miles offshore and north of us, so we weren't in any immediate danger. We reluctantly altered course for Puerto Vallarta, some seventy-five miles away. We had hoped to get at least as far as Cabo San Lucas, but with low fuel, it would have been risky. It was dark when we got close to Cabo Corrientes; it has a lighthouse, but the light frequency didn't match the chart. Shore lights assured us that we were heading into Bahía de Banderas and the Puerto Vallarta inner harbour, where we arrived at 0900 hours. At this point, we had gone 2,060 miles from the Panama Canal, not nearly as far as we had hoped in that time.

After fueling up, we tied stern to at the marina, which cost $1.70 for the night; diesel was twenty-eight cents an imperial gallon. Pat and I walked to the Port Captain's office for directions to Customs and Immigration. It was three miles away, so we kept walking. Two friendly attractive girls in their twenties from California stopped and picked us up in their Jeep and drove us into town. What a kind gesture! Immediately after completing our paperwork, we bused back to the Port Captain's office then took a taxi back to the boat. After straightening out the boat and hanging things to dry, we decided to taxi into town and look around. Jennifer was feeling a lot better but chose to stay behind and read.

We walked the boardwalk along the water and stopped for lunch at Los Palmos where the food was delicious but very hot and spicy, and probably not the best thing for my upset digestive system. Julie bought some bangles and postcards; we stopped at the post office then hailed a taxi to take us home.

After having the best sleep in a long time, we departed at 0730 hours with light winds, under full main and the 180 genoa. It picked up in the afternoon, but we could still keep a full main and the lapper. We saw a pilot whale about fifteen feet long. Then it wasn't long before we saw another one. Soon after, we saw a blue marlin about eight feet long. By doing our watches in the cockpit, we were seeing a lot of wildlife and noticed a lot more phosphorescence in the Pacific; our wake was lit up for sixty feet. When approached by porpoises, it looked like we were being torpedoed.

The next day, winds were hard on the nose from the west. We were trying to work our way west to comfortably sail into Cabo St Lucas. We couldn't rely on our self-steering when so hard on the wind. We had to man the helm day and night. We were about twenty-two degrees north latitude, two thirds across the Sea of Cortez, so still south of the sun by two degrees. It was very difficult to get an accurate sighting when it was almost directly overhead. We kept dead reckoning and expected to see Cabo by mid-afternoon the next day. As the day progressed, so did the wind. We could still stay on a port tack, but we were burying the rail on the starboard side so much that water was coming in the bathroom basin. Pat shut off the valve to it and to the toilet. Because the ship's head was on the starboard side, it was often under water.

We all sat in the cockpit on the port side and had quite a talk. *Why were we doing this?* Had we not been so eager to get to Victoria to begin our new life, we would have headed for Hawaii. We would have had more favourable winds and no current once we were north of the tropical storm region. The four of us agreed that this was what we had to do, which released the tension and made us laugh.

At dusk, things hadn't improved. The rub rail on the starboard side worked its way loose and was slapping against the hull. It had to be tied, which Pat did with the deck under water. The waves were crashing into the sail, tearing the leech of the main. The lapper had torn along the seam for two feet. I was trying to sew it, but under such conditions, it was virtually impossible. Pat hanked on the trysail and the storm jib but dropped an empty sail bag overboard in the process. It certainly wasn't worth trying to recover it.

All of this took place in the dark of night. Fortunately, we had worked our way west over the last couple of days for a comfortable approach to Cabo, or as comfortable as could be with 40-knot winds. We were able to reach off a little, which helped considerably. The temperature was fifty-four degrees Fahrenheit, but after the heat we had been experiencing, it felt freezing, especially when soaking wet.

We could make out the lights at Cabo but realized that it was the hotels. The harbour was just to the east. We reached the harbour at 2200 hours and it was a relief to drop anchor. There were two boats anchored: *Big Mike*, which was a power boat, and a sailboat. It was too late to socialize, and the lights were out on both.

The next morning, June 20, we were up at 0700 hours to survey the damage. The lower lockers on the starboard side were soaked with oily water and not pleasant to clean up. I made pancakes, which picked up our spirits, and we weighed anchor at 0900 hours.

Once out of the lee of Sugar Loaf Mountain, we got nailed by pounding seas and heavy spray. Winds were 25 knots right on the nose. It took two hours to get around the Cape and abeam of the light, a distance of only four miles. Then the winds dropped to about 15 knots, and the seas calmed.

As it got light, we could see shore. Winds had subsided so we were motor sailing. That first day of summer was fifty-four degrees Fahrenheit. Having passed directly under the sun, it would now rise south of us. We had become accustomed to seeing it in the north at noon. With winds right on the nose, we decided to put in at Punta Tosca for a bit of a break. We had been beating our brains out for the last two days and were barely 150 miles from Cabo. We hoped things would improve the next day, but they didn't. We were off at 0700 hours, progressing slowly along the coast. Seals came out to great us from their resting spot. We also saw a lot of krill that we hadn't seen before.

With lots of identifying points on the land, it was easy navigating, but the results were discouraging. We were averaging about 3.7 knots motoring into the wind. The next morning, we tacked back and forth and shut off the motor to save gas. We spent the day under reefed main and lapper on each tack. We were doing 6 or 6.5 knots but not in the direction we wanted. By nightfall, we started the motor, altering course to clear Abreojos, a point of land jutting out to sea.

By early morning, we had cleared the point. I was watching porpoises in our bow wave when suddenly a grey whale, about twice the length of our boat, dove in front of us, leaving a huge swilling slick that we crossed over. It was quite a thrill because grey whales are seldom seen in the Atlantic, where they have almost been whaled into extinction. In the Pacific, they spawn in Scammon's Lagoon in the Sea of Cortez, named after Charles Scammon, a whaler in the mid-1850s. After his success as a whaler almost drove the grey whale into extinction, he had a change of heart and fought for their protection. Now Scammon Lagoon is an important habitat for the reproduction and wintering of these marvelous creatures. His book, *The Marine Mammals of the Northwestern Coast of North America*, written in1874, is a classic. I read it when we first arrived in British Columbia after a close encounter with a grey whale while out in a small row boat. It scared the living daylights out of me and motivated me to study whales, starting with Scammon's book. In fact, when we lived in Whitby, I had given a presentation about whales to a kids' class at the public library.

It was our best day yet because we had light winds and flat seas. Julie made Melissa Fudge, while Pat baked her beer bread, which has that wonderful aroma. By late afternoon, it was back to the usual: howling wind in our teeth and an average of 3 knots. Just after midnight, we could see the halo over Turtle Bay. It was still dark when we arrived at the entrance, so we hove to for two hours before feeling confident enough to enter the harbour. Steve aboard a wooden 30-footer, was the only other boat in the harbour. We slept for a couple of hours, had something to eat, and then headed into the fuel dock. Diesel cost eighty cents per gallon, quite a jump from the twenty cents earlier. Back at anchor, the girls borrowed Steve's dinghy and rowed into shore, while I changed the oil and oil filter and cleaned the fuel filter, and Pat repaired our flags. We invited Steve over for dinner. He was waiting for crew to help him sail to Los Angeles. His motor would only go 3 knots, so he was going to have to sail the whole way. I got on the Maritime Marine Net and was able to pick up someone from LA who patched in a phone call to Steve's parents.

We departed Turtle Bay at 0530 hours under an overcast sky. There was no wind, but the swell from the north-west was slowing us down. After clearing the lee of Cedros Island, we started getting 20 - to 30-knot winds, which continued all day and well into the night. I stayed up all night, being uncomfortable so close to the windward side of the Baja Peninsula. When Pat took over at daybreak, I went down below to rest but not for long; about 0830 hours, Pat yelled for me to come up. There was a large tuna boat approaching us. The captain said he had a man on board who had been shipwrecked and could we take him north as they was going south. They lowered a dinghy over the side and brought him over to us. Even before he arrived, I called the Coast Guard in Long Beach to explain the situation. They said they would stand by and for me to get back to them with details as soon as possible.

He introduced himself as Charles Bobbitt and told us that he had run aground close to shore and had hidden all his possessions in shore amongst the trees. He didn't feel it was necessary to inform the Coast Guard, but I said that I already had and they were waiting for details. He claimed his boat didn't have a name but was thirty feet long. I told the Coast Guard the details and said I would drop him off at San Quentin. That must have made him a bit nervous, but I was referring to the little Mexican town, not the prison. As it turned out, by the time we got there, we couldn't risk making a landfall due to fog. That meant we had to carry on to Ensenada. Conditions were not that great throughout the day, variable winds but heavy seas. Early evening, a grey whale came very close and blew, spraying us. I felt I could have reached out and touched him, he was so close. After doing three shallow dives, he swung behind us and disappeared.

It was rough throughout the night with winds in the 20-knot range against us. Water was coming in the stovepipe, leaking through the window and the hatches. It was miserable! We gave Charles the forward V birth, and the girls slept in the main cabin when they weren't accompanying us on watch. Needless to say, we didn't get Charles to do any watches, as he had already proven his inability to do that on his boat. We confirmed our position at 1500 hours, estimating that it would be 0130 hours when we reached Ensenada.

Just when I thought that things couldn't get any worse, they did. Number two fuel tank ran dry before I realized it in time to engage number three tank. That meant bleeding the air out of the fuel line in such horrific conditions. I did that by turning the engine over with the starter until fuel came out. The starter was dead and didn't turn over. I had a crank for emergency starts, but because the engine was low in the engine compartment, there wasn't enough swing room. Over the next two hours, I lowered the main, swung the boom amidships, and with the boomvang, hoisted the engine up until there was enough clearance that I could swing the crank. This was only possible because I had used universal joints on the prop shaft. I had to reduce the compression to allow me to turn it over fast enough to get fuel flowing. Eventually, I was able to get it started.

Abeam of Ensenada, I determined heavy fog made it too risky to try to make landfall. That meant another day to reach San Diego. I had called the Coast Guard each day to inform them of our position, explaining that I would be taking Charles to San Diego and expected it would be about 1100 hours the next day.

Winds subsided by morning, and we motored for the last stretch to San Diego. I pulled in to the police dock at 1115 hours, but before they arrived, Charles hopped off the bow and was gone. He had promised Pat that he would take us all for dinner after he got some money from the bank. *Gee, what a surprise that we never saw him again!* After much questioning by the police – who were extremely polite – we cleared customs, obtained a cruising permit, kissed the ground, and got back to the boat. Thank goodness for the ham radio, as we were way beyond the range of our VHF most of the time.

The next day was spent mostly on boat maintenance: changing the engine oil and filter, changing oil in the transmission, and fixing the starter. We rented a car and took our poor tattered main in for repairs and did some shopping for the next leg.

We went to the zoo, while Jennifer stayed to finish her final school assignment. She was a little behind because Julie was able to do school work on passages, but Jennifer wasn't. When we returned, we fueled up, topped up our water tanks, and departed at 2300 hours, in calm seas and no wind. There was no moon either, but navigating was simple with the well-lit shoreline.

By 1145 hours the next morning, July 4, we were abeam of Catalina Island, having averaged 5.6 knots motoring from San Diego. At noon we spotted seven killer whales that put on a bit of a show for us. We had hoped we would see the July 4th fireworks in the evening, but we were too far offshore. Winds picked up, so it was a joy to shut off the engine and get back to sailing. Over the next three days, winds were mostly 20 to 30 knots against us, causing choppy seas. We appeared to be fighting a current as well and only averaged 3.5 knots crossing Monterey Bay. Fighting current and wind, we expected to reach San Francisco late evening. As we got close, we saw a few sunfish or mola mola, as they are called locally, and also sighted a large colony of sea lions on a rocky island.

By 2000 hours, we could see the Golden Gate Bridge, but it was three hours before we passed under it. Immediately, we were approached by a large Coast

Guard vessel. With a loud hailer, they instructed us to heave to and prepare to be boarded. They were very polite but suspicious of us when I told them our last port was San Diego. I think they were from the prairies and hadn't really considered that a sailboat could continue through the night without anchoring. While I was showing one of them my log, another was searching, including looking in the kids' lipstick tubes. They were thorough but extremely courteous. The whole operation took well over an hour. Once they gave us the okay and wished us farewell, we docked at the Sausalito Yacht Club. I knew my mother and stepfather were somewhere in San Francisco, but we hadn't made arrangements to meet. I expected they would get in touch with the Coast Guard, who would put out a call for us. Also, we knew Sally was here visiting her uncle and was waiting to hear from us.

Even though it was after 0200 hours when we got to bed, we were up by 0800, had breakfast, registered with the yacht club, and I decided to walk to the nearest spot to pick up a newspaper. I had just passed a phone booth when I heard my mother call out, "Bill." She was just about to call the Coast Guard. What a surprise! She and George had found a campground not four blocks away, guessing that I would come into Sausalito. We had a great reunion! The last time we saw them was in Trinity Bay when we sailed out the St Laurence River, over three years ago.

We were able to contact Sally who joined us, and we all went back to her uncle's home for dinner. We had a ten-day layover. San Francisco has remained one of my favourite cities. Julie and I had got into the habit of going for a run each morning whenever we had a layover, so we carried on our routine for ten days. I did the usual boat maintenance; changed the oil, and scrubbed the bottom. Our mainsail was looking pretty tattered, so I bought a new one readymade from a nearby sail maker that only required a little modification. A local radio station asked me to do an interview, which I did over the telephone. It saved me going downtown to the station.

We met an engaging couple at the marina, who invited us to their home for a wine tasting and dinner. Their friend and her two sons were vintners. Pat enjoyed their cabernet and chardonnay. I enjoyed their pâté and cheese.

Just as the tide was receding at 2200 hours, we reluctantly left family and new friends to begin the last leg of our journey. We passed under the Golden Gate Bridge, and followed the coast in light winds and flat seas under motor.

It was calm all night and well into the next day before we picked up enough winds to sail. By 1700 hours, we were abeam of Point Arena Lighthouse. We were having a shark evening! Dozens of them – ranging from three to eight feet – were just calmly swimming around; they didn't appear to be in an eating frenzy. I'm sure our experiences with turtles, snakes, and porpoises would have been just as common in the Atlantic, but we hadn't spent that much time in the cockpit. Sailing along close to the shore necessitated us to keep a constant watch from the cockpit.

It was foggy the next morning, with less than half a mile visibility. Our dead reckoning position put us close to abeam of Punta Gorda. Late in the afternoon, we bore off to the east towards Crescent City and had a very uncomfortable sail through the night. Pat and I did the watches, giving the girls a break. We were very close to shore but couldn't see it; this required extreme concentration, listening for breaking waves. We were greeted with more fog next morning and couldn't see land. When we spotted a fishing boat, we got a position from him and were disappointed to find that we were well short of the mark.

It was 1100 hours before we entered the harbour at Crescent City. The town had suffered severe devastation in 1964 from tsunamis generated by the Alaskan Good Friday earthquake. Fishing is the major industry, and the harbour was full of fishing boats. Pat and Julie took off to find the Port Captain, while I stayed behind to repair a leaking fuel pump. Moored just ahead of us was a Vancouver 40, *Windy*, from San Francisco, with skipper Warren Glaze and his wife Dee. We dined together that night, and when they took us fishing the next day, we jigged for black cod and caught enough for dinner. Although we only spent a day with them, we became good friends. In fact, the following year, they visited us in Victoria.

We departed via St. George's Channel by 0530 the next morning. Winds picked up to 30 knots, and the seas were huge. It was disappointing because we were focused on getting to Victoria, and it looked like we would have to put in to Brookings, a small Oregon town. It was blinding fog, but we stumbled on the outer buoy to the harbour. I called the Coast Guard for directions for entering the harbour. In seven tortuous hours, we had only covered twenty-five miles.

Brookings gained notoriety during World War II when a Japanese aircraft launched from a submarine, bombed the coastal forest in an effort to set a massive fire; however, it was quickly extinguished. Apart from Pearl Harbour, this was the only other Japanese invasion of the US.

It was 0545 when we pulled away from the dock to face another grueling day. There was no wind to start with, but the lumpy seas were causing Pat to get seasick. That is so often the case when you don't have the steadying effect of the wind in the sails. As the day progressed, so did the wind. In fact it picked up to 40 knots, with gusts to 50 in the afternoon. It was a busy day tacking back and forth, reefing the main once then twice, then finally the trysail. I kept the motor running to give us that extra punch through the waves. I manned the helm the whole day to ensure that we got the most out of each tack. Pat was still suffering down below, the girls braced themselves in the V berth, and I got soaked and cold in the cockpit. I didn't eat all day.

It was such a relief when we dropped anchor in Port Oxford at 1900 hours. After such a dreadful day, we had only covered forty-five miles, averaging 3.4 knots. Even at anchor, the wind kept howling. Julie made us hamburgers, Pat a salad, and Jennifer baked a cake. With the heater going full blast and the oven on, it actually was toasty warm, and cozy. We all sat around discussing whether this had been the worst day since the Panama Canal. It was unanimous that it was. We decided we needed a rest and would lay over for a day and try to dry things. There were two fishing boats and a sailboat anchored so we exchanged greetings with them all from the cockpit.

The next morning, bacon and eggs never tasted so good. Although it had been designated a day of rest, I spent the day repairing the Autohelm, repairing the navigation lights, and getting the depth sounder working. Pat spent the whole day repairing our courtesy flags. It was customary for a ship to fly all the courtesy flags of nations she had visited on reaching the journey's end. Pat was making sure that we made a grand entrance to Victoria's inner harbour. The girls tidied up and hung things out to dry. We bid farewell to our neighbouring sailboat that departed midday with their two young children for the San Juan Islands, but not before the skipper had to jump overboard to untangle his anchor rode from around the propeller.

We weighed anchor at 0500 hours in flat calm, with only slight 10 to 15 knot breezes. We were hard on the wind but didn't need the motor. Even against the current, we were averaging 5.5 knots. We ducked into Coos Bay, Oregon, at 1500 hours. Pat went into town to pick up engine oil and clear customs, returning with fish and chips. I changed the oil and filter. After only three hours, we headed out to sea again. It was our plan to carry on to Neah Bay, which was about three days away. Seas were comfortable and winds continued light, but it was very foggy. Julie baked hot cross buns for us, and Pat and I both stayed on watch in the cockpit because visibility was down to a quarter of a mile.

We worked our way offshore to stay well clear of the Columbia River outfall. By evening, we were running out of wind and started the engine. Being so foggy, we had to rely on sound to warn of waves breaking on rocks, yet with the engine running, it was difficult to hear. At midnight, Julie saved the day when she sensed that the exhaust note had changed. It was quickly revealed that the water pump belt had broken and the engine was overheating. Fortunately, it hadn't run long enough to do any damage. I had the unpleasant task of installing the spare belt in rolling seas. At sea, a fifteen-minute job takes about an hour and a half. Also, I had to figure out why the alarm wasn't working.

We were focused on finding Cape Flattery. Once identified, we would bear to starboard to enter the Juan de Fuca Strait. Then Neah Bay would only be seven miles away. We had to dodge dozens of seiners fishing at the mouth of the Strait. They had strobe lights on floats marking the end of their nets, which we had to pick our way through. Finally, we picked up the whistle buoy identifying the cape. By 0830 we edged into the fuel dock at Neah Bay. I had called the Coast Guard in Victoria, notifying them of an arrival time of 1100 hours the next day. Now we had to figure out what time to leave Neah Bay to meet that deadline. It would be about twelve hours, so we had the day to arrange things then leave at 2200 hours for the final leg of our journey.

Sitting in the cockpit by myself, it suddenly occurred to me that our epic journey would come to an end the following day. Since traversing the Panama Canal, we had often had conversations about reaching Victoria, but this time, I was alone and overcome with emotion. In fact, it brought tears to my eyes. I thought of all the close calls we had endured; the fear, the near disasters, the excitement and joy of our many landfalls. I just felt so grateful for the experiences I had enjoyed with the closeness of my family. I had fulfilled a dream, one many have had I'm sure. I don't know if anyone heard me, but through tears I said, "I'm a pretty lucky guy!"

In the black of night, we crossed the shipping lanes of the Juan de Fuca Strait to the south side of Vancouver Island and worked our way along the coast. We were a little early when we fetched the entrance to Victoria's Inner Harbour, so we hove to, strung our thirty-four courtesy flags up the forestay to the masthead, down the backstay to the stern rail, then the yellow quarantine flag up to the starboard spreader complying with the custom to fly all the courtesy flags of the countries one has visited when you make the final landfall.

For the last few days of our journey, we all had anxious questions. *Where will we live? What school will the girls go to? Will I find a job?* Fortunately, the excitement of beginning our new life outweighed these fears.

It was July 30, 1982, and after three years at sea, we had completed our 26,000 nautical mile adventure. After clearing customs and immigration, we were greeted by a TV crew and friends with a large bottle of champagne.

The glamorous Empress Hotel was dead ahead. The stately Legislative Buildings were off to starboard.

We were home!

Glossary of Sailing Terms

- Aft: toward the stern.
- Anchor rode: line (rope) or chain from anchor to boat.
- Athwart ship: perpendicular to the centre line of the boat.
- Backstay: a line supporting the mast from aft.
- Beaufort scale: forces 1 to 12 to describe wind conditions. Force 1 would be calms seas and gentle wind. Force 12 is hurricane winds of 70 knots or more. A system developed in 1830 by Sir Francis Beaufort.
- Bollard: item to fasten a line on (either on a dock or a boat).
- Bow: front of the ship.
- Bowsprit: a spar or pole extending forward on the bow and is an anchor point for a stay.
- Boomvang: a line running through blocks to pull down the boom to tighten up the luff of the mainsail especially when running.
- Cardinal Beacon: used in conjunction with the compass to indicate where the mariner may find the safe navigable water. It is placed in one of the four quadrants (North, East, South and West), bounded by inter-cardinal bearings from the point marked.
- Cleat: same as a bollard.
- Clew: corners of a sail, usually metal rings for securing sheets.
- Dead reckoning: an estimate of the current position on our chart.
- Fairlead: a line that runs through a block or pulley often feeding jib sheets to a winch.
- Fetch or fetching: arriving at a destination
- Forestay: a line supporting the mast from the bow.
- Gamming: socializing with other yachtsmen.
- Gunnels: the upper edge of the side of a vessel.
- Hank: to attach a sail on a stay or mast.
- Hawser: a large rope for towing, mooring, or securing a ship.

- Hove to: making the boat stationary by back winding the jib.
- Hull speed: roughly 1.35 X the square route of a boats waterline length.
- Jibe: when vessel tacks going downwind.
- Knots: speed; 1 knot is 1.15078 mph.
- Landfall: when a vessel arrives at a destination.
- Nautical mile: 6,076 feet or 1,852 metres compared to a statutory mile, which is 5,289 feet.
- Painter: line or rope on bow of dinghy.
- Port: left side of the ship.
- Porthole: a window in a ship to provide air and light down below. Often round but not always.
- Ratlines or Rattlin's: lines strung between shrouds to facilitate climbing to the spreaders, like a ladder.
- Reef: reduce sail, usually the main by lowering a portion of it.
- Rhumb line: the path of a ship that maintains a fixed compass direction, shown on a chart to a destination.
- Sheets: lines from clew on sail to a fairlead.
- Shrouds: lines on either side of the mast holding it up.
- Spreaders: horizontal supports on the mast athwart ship, usually at the top third or higher of the mast.
- Splicing rope: often to make an eye or join two pieces of rope.
- Stay: a line supporting the mast fore and aft (forestay/backstay).
- Starboard or starbr'd: the right side of the ship.
- Stern: rear or back of the ship.
- Weigh anchor: hoist up an anchor.
- Whipping rope: binding around the end of rope to prevent it from fraying.

About The Author

Having been diagnosed with hepatitis, Bill Hapgood was faced with the prospect of death, which made him wonder, what is life's journey all about? With a will to survive, his recovery had given him a new zest for life, and one that would take him and his young family on an amazing voyage, covering 26,000 nautical miles of ocean.

Born in Quebec, Bill's sea adventures began with a three-month sailing excursion from Vancouver to Alaska, which was the inspiration to what would become the start of a three-year sailing voyage. Having spent many years racing cars, in 1970 he became a champion in Production Sports Car Racing. However, it was sailing and camping with his family that led him to write this book, memories of *Three Years at Sea*, which follows the family of four (including two young daughters) on their voyage aboard their twenty-nine foot sailboat, while solely reliant on a sextant and compass for navigation. Throughout their journey Bill kept daily ship logs, which would prove to serve him well in terms of all the research needed to write his book.

Printed in Canada